VISION AND PROPHECY
IN AMOS

1955 FACULTY LECTURES
BAPTIST THEOLOGICAL SEMINARY
RÜSCHLIKON/ZH, SWITZERLAND

BY

JOHN D. W. WATTS

Wm. B. Eerdmans Publishing Company
Grand Rapids, Michigan

TABLE OF CONTENTS

ABBREVIATIONS

A.J.S.L.:	*The American Journal of Semitic Languages and Literature* (Chicago).
A.J.T.:	*The American Journal of Theology* (Chicago).
A.N.E.T.:	*Ancient Near Eastern Texts* (ed. Pritchard, Princeton, 1950).
A.O.:	*Der Alte Orient* (Leipzig).
A.R.V.	*American Revised Version of the Bible* (N.Y., 1901).
A.R.W.:	*Archiv für Religionswissenschaft* (Freiburg i. Br.).
A.T.:	*American Translation of the Bible* (Chicago, 1935).
A.T.D.:	*Das Alte Testament Deutsch* (Göttingen).
A.T.R.:	*The Anglican Theological Review* (N.Y.).
A.T.A.N.T.:	*Abhandlungen zur Theologie des Alten und Neuen Testaments* (Zürich).
A.V.	*Authorized Version of the Bible.*
B.A.S.O.R.:	*The Bulletin of the American Schools of Oriental Research* (Baltimore).
B.B.B.:	*Bonner Biblische Beiträge.*
B.Ev.T.:	*Beiheft zur "Evangelische Theologie"* (München).
B.F.:	*Festschrift für Alfred Bertholet* (Tübingen, 1950).
B.J.R.L.:	*Bulletin of the John Rylands Library* (Manchester).
B.W.A.N.T.:	*Beiträge zur Wissenschaft vom Alten und Neuen Testament* (Stuttgart).
B.Z.A.W.:	*Beihefte zur Zeitschrift für die alttestamentliche Wissenschaft* (Berlin).
C.B.:	*Cambridge Bible for Schools and Colleges.*
C.M.:	G. R. Driver, *Canaanite Myths and Legends* (Edinburgh, 1956).
E.B.:	*Encyclopedia Biblica* (London, 1899).
Ev.T.:	*Evangelische Theologie* (München).
Ex.T.:	*The Expository Times* (Edinburgh).
Exp.:	*The Expositor* (London).
H.T.R.:	*Harvard Theological Review* (Cambridge, Mass.).
H.U.C.A.:	*Hebrew Union College Annual* (Cincinnati).
I.B.:	*The Interpreter's Bible* (N.Y., 1951-57).
I.C.C.:	*International Critical Commentary* (Edinburgh).
J.B.L.:	*Journal of Biblical Literature* (Philadelphia).
J.M.E.O.S.:	*Journal of the Manchester Egyptian and Oriental Society.*
J.N.E.S.:	*Journal of Near Eastern Studies* (Chicago).
J.S.S.:	*Journal of Semitic Studies* (Manchester).
J.T.S.:	*Journal of Theological Studies* (Oxford).
K.A.T.:	*Kommentar zum Alten Testament* (ed. Sellin, Leipzig).
K.S.:	A. Alt, *Kleine Schriften zur Geschichte des Volkes Israel*, 2 vols. (München, 1953).
M.G.W.J.:	*Monatschrift für die Geschichte und Wissenschaft des Judentum* (Breslau).
N.T.T.:	*Norsk Teologisk Tidsskrift* (Oslo).
N.K.Z.:	*Neue Kirchliche Zeitschrift* (*Leipzig*).
O.T.M.S.:	*The Old Testament and Modern Study* (ed. H. H. Rowley, Oxford, 1951).
O.T.S.	*Oudtestamentische Studien* (Leiden).
P.E.Q.:	*Palestine Exploration Quarterly* (London).
P.J.B.:	*Palästina Jahrbuch* (Berlin).
P.S.:	S. Mowinckel, *Psalmenstudien* (Christiana, 1921-24)
R.B.:	*Revue Biblique* (Paris).

R.G.G.:	*Religion in Geschichte und Gegenwart* (2nd ed., Tübingen, 1927); (3rd ed., Tübingen, 1956).
R.H.P.R.:	*Revue d'histoire et de philosophie religieuse* (Strasbourg).
R.R.:	*Record and Revelation* (ed. H. W. Robinson, Oxford, 1938).
R.S.V.:	*The Revised Standard Version of the Bible* (N.Y., 1952).
S.A.T.:	*Schriften des Alten Testaments* (Göttingen).
S.B.U.:	*Svenskt Bibliskt Uppslagsverk* (Stockholm, 1948-52).
S.E.Å.:	*Svensk Exegetisk Årsbok* (Uppsala).
S.H.R.:	*Studies in History and Religion*: H. W. Robinson Festschrift (ed. E. A. Payne, London, 1942).
S.J.T.:	*Scottish Journal of Theology* (Edinburgh).
S.L.:	H. H. Rowley, *The Servant of the Lord* (London, 1952).
S.O.T.P.:	*Studies in Old Testament Prophecy*: T. H. Robinson Festschrift (ed. H. H. Rowley, Edinburgh, 1950).
S.T.:	*Studia Theologica* (Lund).
S.T.U.:	*Schweizerische Theologische Umschau* (Bern).
S.V.K.:	*Skrifter Videnskabsselskabet i Kristiania.*
S.V.T.	*Supplement to Vetus Testamentum* (Leiden).
T.R.:	*Theologische Rundschau* (Tübingen).
T.W.N.T.:	*Theologisches Wörterbuch zum Neuen Testament* (Stuttgart, 1932).
T.L.Z.:	*Theologische Literaturzeitung* (Berlin).
U.H.:	C. H. Gorden, *Ugaritic Handbook* (Rome, 1947).
U.L.:	C. H. Gorden, *Ugaritic Literature* (Rome, 1949).
U.U.Å.:	*Uppsala Universitets Årsskrift.*
V.T.:	*Vetus Testamentum* (Leiden).
W.C.:	*Westminster Commentaries* (London).
W.H.A.:	*Westminster Historical Atlas to the Bible* (2nd ed., Philadelphia, 1956).
W.O.:	*Die Welt des Orients* (Göttingen).
Z.A.W.:	*Zeitschrift für die alttestamentliche Wissenschaft* (Berlin).
Z.S.T.:	*Zeitschrift für systematische Theologie* (Berlin).
Z.T.K.:	*Zeitschrift für Theologie und Kirche* (Tübingen).
Z.W.T.:	*Zeitschrift für wissenschaftliche Theologie* (Leipzig).

CHAPTER ONE

WHAT KIND OF PROPHET WAS AMOS?

Through most of the history of the Christian Church scholars have concerned themselves very little with the *prophets* as persons. Their interest has, insofar as they have dealt with the Old Testament, centered in the *prophecies* from which they could draw proofs that Jesus was Messiah.[1] Since all the Old Testament was viewed as "prophetic", even the distinction between the strictly prophetic and other books was largely overlooked. Because of this heavy emphasis upon messianic proof-texts, personality and historical setting fell into oblivion. The prophetic writings were viewed as unique in the sense that all Scripture was unique. But almost the only distinguishing mark observed in them was that more messianic references were to be found there.

The advent of critical study in the 18th century with its delineation of historical background as a necessary prerequisite to interpretation drew attention *again* to the prophets themselves.[2] "Again" because it

---

[1] Cf. H. D. F. Sparks, *The Old Testament in the Christian Church* (London, 1944), p. 23; N. W. Porteous, "Prophecy," *R.R.*, p. 248, "Time was when the importance of Hebrew prophecy lay almost entirely in the so-called Messianic prophecies which the prophetic books contained." For a parallel contemporary interpretation, see B. Ramm, *Protestant Biblical Interpretation* (Boston, 1950), p. 155 ff. For a survey and analysis of this view, see K. Fullerton, *Prophecy and Authority* (N.Y., 1919). In referring to the earlier biblical theology of the 19th century, H. E. Dana, *Searching the Scriptures* (New Orleans, 1936), p. 76 says, "... the method by which (scripture references) are employed is almost wholly deductive, and no notice whatever is taken of the historical perspective in the teaching of the Bible." An excellent general presentation of the problem may be found in R. M. Grant, *The Bible in the Church* (New York, 1948) and the older W. R. Smith, *The Prophets of Israel* (2nd ed., London, 1895), p. 5 f.

[2] Books on prophecy in the 19th century are legion. See the bibliography in A. B. Davidson, *Old Testament Prophecy* (Edinburgh, 1903). But even when they discuss messianic prophecy (Briggs, Stanton, Delitzsch, Volz, Hühn, Kittel, and Riehm), it is evident that all show greater consideration for the persons and history related to prophecy. The works of Kuenen, G. A. Smith, Giesebrecht, Cornill, Wellhausen, Duhm, Gunkel, J. M. P. Smith, and T. H. Robinson have given the greatest impetus to the portrayal of the prophets as individuals. As a result today there is a wealth of biographical treatments of the prophets and every other study of prophecy pays respect to the biographical element.

is obvious that those who recorded and transmitted the Old Testament literature took pains to preserve biographical material. [1] With this interest in historical background and person came a variety of descriptions often formed in reaction to the extreme emphasis upon the predictive element. Prophets were pictured as religious geniuses,[2] creators of ethical religion, [3] religious reformers, [4] or as preachers of social righteousness. [5] A prophet was defined as one who "spoke for God." [6] He was viewed as something quite new in history and unique in Israel. The prophet was accorded the honor of being the original exponent of "ethical monotheism." [7]

In the twentieth century study of the prophets has come into its own. [8] By showing that the phenomena was not exclusively Israelite in form or origin, [9] two methods of study have emphasized what Old

---

[1] Particularly the prophetic biographies of Elijah and Elisha (I Kings 17-II Kings 13) and the many shorter accounts in the prophetic books as well as those biographical sections of the Latter Prophets.

[2] Cf. T. J. Meek, *Hebrew Origins* (2nd ed. New York, 1950), p. 178 and others.

[3] L. Waterman, "The Ethical Clarity of the Prophets," *J.B.L.* LXIV (1945), p. 301 and others. E. Troeltsch, "Das Ethos der hebräischen Propheten," *Logos* VI (1916-17), p. 1 ff.

[4] T. H. Robinson, *Prophecy and the Prophets* (London, 1923), p. 60 and others.

[5] S. A. Cook, *The Truth of the Bible* (London, 1938), p. 30 f. and others.

[6] H. P. Smith, *Essays on Biblical Interpretation* (London, 1921), p. 176 and others. Cf. D. Lattes, "Amos: prophète de la justice," *Madregoth* I (1940).

[7] J. Morgenstern, "Amos Studies I," *H.U.C.A.* XI (1936), p. 53; and R. S. Cripps, *A Critical and Exegetical Commentary on the Book of Amos* (London, 1929; 2nd ed., 1955), p. 29.

[8] Recent reviews of literature and current opinions may be found in N. W. Porteous, "Prophecy," *R.R.*, pp. 216-249; H.-H. Rowley, "The Nature of Old Testament Prophecy in the Light of Recent Study," *H.T.R.* XXXVIII (1945), pp. 1-38 and reprinted in H. H. Rowley, *The Servant of the Lord* (London, 1952), pp. 89-128; O. Eissfeldt, "The Prophetic literature," *O.T.M.S.*, pp. 115-161; and G. Fohrer, "Neuere Literatur zu den alttestamentlichen Propheten," *T.R.* XX (1952), pp. 193-271 and pp. 295-361.

[9] Ed. Meyer, *Die Israeliten und ihre Nachbarstämme* (Halle, 1906), pp. 451 ff.; H. Gressmann, "Foreign Influences in Hebrew Prophecy," *J.T.S.* XXVII (1926), p. 24ff.; T. H. Robinson, "Die prophetischen Bücher im Lichte neuer Entdeckungen," *Z.A.W.* XLV (1927), p. 3-9; J. H. Breasted, *The Dawn of Conscience* (New York, 1933), p. 363; A. Guillaume, *Prophecy and Divination among Hebrews and other Semites* (London, 1938); W. Zimmerli, *La Prophétie dans l'Ancien Testament et dans l'Islam* (Lausanne, 1945); M. Noth, "History and the Word of God in the Old Testament," *B.J.R.L.* XXXII (1949-50), pp. 194-206; A. Lods, "Une Tablette Inédite de Mari, Interessante pour l'histoire ancienne de prophétisme Sémitique," *S.O.T.P.*, p. 103-110; J. Pedersen, "The Role Played by Inspired Persons among the Israelites and the Arabs," *S.O.T.P.*, pp. 127-142; W. von Soden, *W.O.* I (1950), pp. 397-403; A. Neher, *L'Essence du Prophétisme* (Paris, 1955), pp. 17-81.

Methods of prophetic study:

Testament prophecy had in common with other prophetic movements. One method analyses psychological phenomena and deals with the element of ecstasy.[1] HÖLSCHER's work[2] brought this issue into the foreground so that many of his followers and opponents have used ecstasy as a standard for judging prophecy.[3] The second method sketches the social and religious setting of prophecy, studies it as an institution, and points out the parallel phenomena found in related Near Eastern cultures. Since MOWIN-CKEL's epochal work,[4] this relation to cult and ritual has become a common criterion for evaluating prophecy while the function and form of cult-prophecy have been heatedly discussed.[5] Both of these methods in the very nature of the case stress features which all hold

---

[1] Ecstasy has been defined in a variety of ways. It is used by some to describe experiences defined as "mystical," while others restrict it to more violent displays of abnormal psychical obsession.

[2] G. HÖLSCHER, *Die Propheten* (Göttingen, 1917).

[3] W. JACOBI, *Die Ekstase der alttestamentlichen Propheten* (Munich, 1920); T. H. ROBINSON, "The Ecstatic Element in Old Testament Prophecy," *Expositor* 8th series (1921); L. P. HORST, "L'extase chez les prophètes d'Israel d'après les travaux HÖLSCHER et de GUNKEL," *R.H.P.R.* II (1922), pp. 337-348; T. H. ROBINSON, *Prophecy and the Prophets in Ancient Israel* (London, 1923); H. W. HERZBERG, *Prophet und Gott* (1923); H. W. HINES, "The Prophet as a Mystic," *A.J.S.L.* XL (1923-24), p. 37ff.; J. LINDBLOM, *Die literarische Gattung der prophetischen Literatur* (Uppsala, 1924); M. D. R. WILLINK, *The Prophetic Consciousness* (London, 1924); N. MICHLEM, *Prophecy and Eschatology* (London, 1926), p. 50; T. H. ROBINSON, "Die prophetischen Bücher im Lichte neuer Entdeckungen," *Z.A.W.* XLV (1927), pp. 3-9; H. W. HINES, "The Development of the Psychology of Prophecy," *Journal of Religion* VIII (1928), p. 212 ff.; J. LINDBLOM, *Profetismen i Israel* (Uppsala, 1934); H. HACKMANN, "Die geistigen Abnormalitäten der alttestamentlichen Propheten," *N.T.T.* XXIII (1934), pp. 23-48; S. MOWIN-CKEL, "Ecstatic Experience and Rational Elaboration in Old Testament Prophecy," *A.O.* XIII (1935), p. 273 note; A. LODS, *The Prophets and the Rise of Judaism* (London, 1937), p. 51 ff.; J. MAUCHLINE, "Ecstasy," *Ex.T.* XLIX (1937-38), pp. 295-299; PORTEOUS, *op. cit.*, p. 228. Other literature may be found in ROWLEY, *op. cit.*, p. 95; H. KNIGHT, *The Hebrew Prophetic Consciousness* (London, 1947), p. 53 ff.; J. LINDBLOM, "Einige Grundfragen der alttestamentlichen Wissenschaft," *B.F.*, pp. 325-337; R. E. D. CLARK, "Prophecy and Psychical Research," *Journal of the Transactions of the Victoria Institute* LXXXIII (1951), pp. 137-157.

[4] S. MOWINCKEL, *Psalmenstudien III: Die Kultprophetie und prophetische Psalmen* (Oslo, 1923).

[5] S. H. HOOKE, *et al, Myth and Ritual* (London 1933); Id., *The Labyrinth* (London, 1935); A. R. JOHNSON, *The Cult Prophet in Ancient Israel* (Cardiff, 1944); A. HALDAR, *Associations of Cult Prophets among the Ancient Semites* (Uppsala, 1945); I. ENGNELL, "Profetia och Tradition," *Lindblom Festschrift, S.E.Å.* XII (1947), p. 110 ff.; S. JELLICOE, "The Prophets and the Cultus," *Ex. T.* LX (1948-49), pp. 256-258; Y. CHARY, *Le culte dans la littérature prophétique exilienne et postexilienne* (unpublished dissertation: Catholic Theological Faculty, Lyon, 1952).

in common and minimize the unique contributions of Israelitic prophecy.

Against these latter methods has arisen another view of the canonical prophets as heralds of judgement. [1] This feature, it is claimed, distinguishes the canonical prophets from all others both in Israel and outside. [2] Closely related to this view are those works concerned with the problem of true and false prophecy. [3] They, too, stress the uniqueness and newness represented in the Latter Prophets of the Old Testament.

The problem posed by these developments is this: Were the canonical prophets a continuation of the older *nābī'* tradition in Israel? Or were they quite different, representing a new phenomenon in Israel and in the world?

A study of the Book of Amos should make an important contribution to the answer of these questions for he was the first prophet whose words have been recorded. [4] His book is remarkably well-preserved so that such a study does not bog down in textual problems. And the short biographical account in vii 10-17 bears directly on this problem. [5]

---

[1] One common element recognized in this view and that above is that of prediction. Cf. H. GRESSMANN, *Der Messias* (Göttingen, 1929), p. 69; F. C. Synge, "Prophecy and 'Pronouncement'," *Church Quarterly Review* CXXXVI (1943), pp. 36-58; R. DUNKERLEY, "Prophecy and Prediction," *Ebda* LXI (1949-50), pp. 260-263; E. WÜRTHWEIN, Amos Studien I," *Z.A.W.* LXII (1950) p. 26.

[2] B. BAENTSCH, *Z.W.T.* I (1908), p. 464; W. COSSMANN, *Die Entwicklung des Gerichtsgedankens bei den alttestamentlichen Propheten, B.Z.A.W.* XV (Giessen, 1915); GRESSMANN, *op. cit.,* p. 77 ff.; H. GUNKEL, "Propheten Israels seit Amos," *R.G.G.* IV (2nd. ed., 1930), cols. 1538-54; S. MOWINCKEL, *J.B.L.* LIII (1934) p. 219; A. JEPSEN, *Nabi* (Munich, 1934), p. 252; E. WÜRTHWEIN, *op. cit.* pp. 10-52; Id., "Ursprung der prophetischen Gerichtsrede," *Z.T.K.* XLIX (1952), pp. 1-16; F. HESSE, "Wurzelt die prophetische Gerichtsrede in israelitischem Kult?" *Z.A.W.* XLV (1953), pp. 45-52. But some now argue that prophecy includes both judgement and salvation: cf. W. ZIMMERLI, "Gericht und Heil im alttestamentlichen Prophetenwort," *Der Anfang* (1948), pp. 21-46; ROWLEY, *op. cit.,* p. 125.

[3] G. VON RAD, "Falsche Propheten," *Z.A.W.* CI (1933), pp. 109-120; E. F. SIEGMAN, *The False Prophets of the Old Testament* (Washington, 1939); M. BUBER, "Falsche Propheten," *Die Wandlung* II (1946-47), pp. 277-283; K. HARMS, *Die Falschen Propheten* (Göttingen, 1947); G. QUELL, *Wahre und falsche Propheten* (Gütersloh, 1952); A. H. EDELKOORT, "Prophet und Prophet," *O.T.S.* V (1948), pp. 178-189.

[4] Most scholars agree in this opinion. One outstanding exception is N. H. SNAITH, *Mercy and Sacrifice* (London, 1953), who would put Hosea earlier. But note his earlier opinion *Study Notes on Bible Books: Amos I* (London, 1945), p. 48: "In all this (new prophetic contribution) Amos was the pioneer."

[5] Especially through Amos' denial of his right to the title in vii 14.

The larger problem may be restated: What kind of prophet was Amos? Was he a prophet at all?

A. AMOS' BACKGROUND

To understand Amos, the prophet, one must first attempt to know Amos, the man, particularly as he was before he became a prophet. Amos came from Tekoa, [1] a village 18 km. south of Jerusalem (9 km. south and west of Bethlehem) at the edge of the plateau called "the Field." [2] With 850 m. above sea level it was higher than Bethlehem or Jerusalem, and its position overlooking the chasm of the dead sea and the Wilderness of Judea gave it an awesome view toward the East. [3]

Tekoa is mentioned twice in David's history. [4] Rehoboam took advantage of its natural position to fortify it. [5] In the resettlement after the Exile, Tekoa was one of the first villages able to supply aid in rebuilding Jerusalem. [6] Chronicles [7] locates it by inference in Judah, specifically near Ephratha.

Four words describe the original profession and status of Amos. But only one of the four is clear beyond question. Amos claimed that Jahweh took him mē'aḥārē haẓẓōn "from behind (following) the flock." [8] This unquestionably relates to care of sheep. Tekoa's location made it a natural center for sheep-herders. [9]

---

[1] F. M. ABEL, Geographie de la Palestine II (aris, 1938) p. 478; G. A. SMITH, The Historical Geohraphy of the Holy Land (25th ed., London, 1931), p. 314 (also pp. 257, 268, 317); G. DALMAN, P.J.B. IX (1913), p. 29 f.; W. SÜTTERLIN, P.J.B XII (1921), pp. 31-46; Id. P.E.Q. (1929), pp. 171 and 174; W. A. L. ELMSLIE, How Came Our Faith (Cambridge, 1948), p. 245.

[2] Cf. Luke ii 8.

[3] Cf. ELMSLIE, op. cit.

[4] II Sam. xiv 2 and xxiii 26.

[5] II Chronicles xi 6, Jer. vi 1. Cf. A. ALT, "Bemerkungen zu einigen judäischen Ortslisten," K.S. II, p. 290; ABEL, op. cit., p. 86.

[6] Neh. iii and 27. Cf. ALT, "Die Rolle Samarias bei der Entstehung des Judentums," op. cit., p. 335; ABEL, op. cit., p. 121.

[7] ii 19, 24; iv 5. But various rabbinic sources indicate a Galileean location on the basis of these same verses. David Qimchi located it in Asher, Pseudo Epiphanius in Zebulun. Cf. H. SCHMIDT, Budde Festschrift (B.Z.A.W. 34, Giessen, 1920); G. DALMAN, P.J.B. XII (1921), p. 45, n. 2; S. LINDLER "Utsikten präm Tekoa", Festschrift Eric Stave (Uppsala, 1922), pp. 338-40; S. KLEIN, M.G.W.J. LXVII (1923), p. 27 ff.; DALMAN, T.L.Z. XLIX (1924), col. 389; Id., Orte und Wege Jesu (3rd. ed., 1924), p. 209; S. SPEIER, V.T. III (1953), p. 305.

[8] Amos vii 15.

[9] Cf. I Sam. xvi and David. Carmel (I Sam. xxiv) is just to the south. Cf. W.H.A. (1946), Plate VI.

Each of the other three expressions is not without problems. Amos was "one of the *nōqdīm* from Tekoa." [1] The word *nōqēd* appears only once more in the Old Testament: a description of "Mesha, King of Moab." [2] Arabic has a similar word for a particular kind of short-legged sheep and its shepherd. [3] Ugaritic texts have the plural form a number of times indicating particular social or guild groups. [4] Twice it appears in the title of one who is ' Chief of the priests and chief of the *nōqdīm*." [5] This latter usage has led a number of scholars to see some cultic meaning in the word. [6] But they seem to have failed to make their case. The attempt to mediate by saying *nōqēd* is the shepherd of the temple's flocks [7] shows to what lengths some will go to establish a "cultic connection" no matter how thin. The earliest versions were thoroughly confused in translating this word as a short survey would show. [8] Aquila, Cyril, and Symmachus are the first to attempt translation and all have variations of the idea "herder" [9] while the Targum is even more specific with "sheep-master." [10] The word was obviously little-known. But it is clear that it designated a profession. That profession was one of raising and keeping sheep. Amos was "one of the sheep-masters of Tekoa." [11] The next word is *bōqēr*. The form of the word is that of an active

---

[1] Amos i 1.

[2] II Kings iii 4.

[3] نَقَل — a kind of small sheep. نَقَّال a keeper of this kind of sheep.

[4] C. GORDON, *Ugaritic Handbook* (Rome, 1947), Glossary No. 1353: texts cxiii 17; ccc 12; cccviii 12. Also one Hurrian text, iv 38.

[5] Ibid., lxii IV: 53.

[6] I. ENGNELL, *Studies in Divine Kingschip* (Uppsala, 1943), p. 87; A. HALDAR, *Associations of Cult Prophets* (Uppsala, 1945), p. 79, n. 5, and p. 112; Cf. criticisms of E. SJÖBERG, *S.E.Å.* XIV (1949), p. 15 ff.; O. EISSFELDT, *op. cit.*, p. 159; M. Bič, "Der Prophet Amos—ein Haepatoskopos," *V.T.* I (1951), p. 292; A. MURTONEN, "The Prophet Amos—a Hepatoscoper?" *V.T.* II (1952), p. 171.

[7] G. A. DANELL, "Var Amos verkligen en ńābiē?" *S.E.Å.* XVI (1951), pp. 7-20; Cf. SAN NICOLO, *Orientalia* NS 17 (1948), pp. 273-293.

[8] Cf. *Duodecim Prophetae*: *Septuaginta* XIII, ed. J. Ziegler (Göttingen, 1943), p. 180. The basic rendering of the LXX seems to be a corrupt transliteration understood as a place name. Theodocian, followed by Jerome, simply transliterated the Hebrew, as did the Peshitta.

[9] Aquila　　— ἐν ποιμνιοτρόφοις
Cyril　　— οἱ ἕτεροι ἐν τοῖς κτηνοτρόφοις
Symmachus — ἐν τοῖς ποιμέσιν

[10] מרי גיתין. Cf. SPEIER, *op. cit.*; and BIC, *op. cit.*

[11] The conclusion of virtually all the commentaries still stands; Cf. most recently, A. S. KAPELRUD, *Central Ideas in Amos* (Oslo, 1956), p. 6 ff.; O. EISSFELDT, *Einleitung in das Alte Testament* (2nd ed., Tübingen, 1956), p. 483 n. 2.

participle. Usually the verb is construed as built on the noun *bāqăr* which means an ox or bullock, therefore designating one who cares for or raises oxen (Rinderhirt). [1] This would contradict the two designations just discussed, and most such interpreters suggest an emendation to *nōqēd*. [2] The letters are enough alike to make such a corruption easy. [3] But does *bōqēr* need to be viewed as a denominative verb? The basic root appears elsewhere with the simple meaning "to examine carefully, to care for." [4] An active participle from this root would simply mean a "herder" (tender) without designation of the kind of animals cared for. [5] For this word, as well, cultic meaning has been sought. [6] But these cultic designations shatter upon the reference to "the flock" in the next line, [7] while this reference merely strengthens the broader meaning of *bōqēr* here suggested.

These three words give us a clear picture of Amos as one whose profession was the care of sheep. He was not simply a shepherd. He probably owned, [8] raised, [9] cared-for, [10] and dealt in sheep, although we have no way of measuring his wealth or position. [11]

---

[1] KÖHLER-BAUMGARTNER, *Lexicon in Veteris Testamenti Libros* (Leiden, 1953), p. 114; BROWN, DRIVER, and BRIGGS, *Hebrew and English Lexicon of the Old Testament* (Oxford, 1907), p. 133; and most commentaries.

[2] Among the latest are MAAG, CRIPPS, and SNAITH. KÖHLER notes that the beginning of this word's corruption in 1 : 1 is shown in the LXX where *dālēth* has already changed to *rēsh*.

[3] *Nūn* to *bēth*, and *dālēth* to *rēsh*.

[4] Lev. xiii 36. Cf. J. FÜRST, *A Hebrew and Chaldee Lexicon* (3rd ed. English translation, London, 1867), p. 232.

[5] *Ibid.*: "seek in order to care for."

[6] HALDAR, *op. cit.*; BIČ, *op. cit.*; Ibid., *V.T.* IV (1954), p. 413. Note MURTONEN's reply to BIČ (*op. cit.*) which contains the interesting suggestion that the basic meaning is "to bore" in the sense of marking sheep. Other pertinent passages include Prov. xx 25, II Kings xvi 15, and Ps. xxvii; Cf. W. R. SMITH, *The Religion of the Semites* (2nd ed., London, 1907), p. 467; E. KAUTZSCH, *Aramaismen im Alten Testament*, p. 24; P. HAUPT, *Sacred Books of the Old Testament, loc. cit.*; W. R. HARPER, *Amos and Hosea: I.C.C.* (Edinburgh, 1905), p. 171; E. HAMMERSHAIMB, *Amos* (Copenhagen, 1946), p. 116 seems to say that the term may apply to a tender of either sheep or cattle. Cf. H. SCHMIDT, *Das Gebet der Angeklagten* (B.Z.A.W. XLIX, Giessen, 1928), p. 27, n. 2.

[7] Cf. Ez. xxxiv 11-12 where a *Piel* form of בלר is used with צאן. LXX translates αἰπόλος—goatherd. So Jewish Tradition's "sheepmaster"; CRIPPS, *op. cit.*, p. 10; SNAITH, *Study Notes on Bible Books: Amos, Part II* (London, 1946), p. 126.

[8] NOWACK, *Die kleinen Propheten* (3rd. ed., Göttingen, 1922), p. 118; SELLIN, *Das Zwölf Propheten Buch* (3rd. ed., Leipzig, 1929), p. 196.

[9] MAAG, *Text Amos*, p. 2.

[10] H. E. W. FOSBROKE, *I.B.* VI (N.Y., 1956), p. 763; HARPER, *op. cit.*, p. 2.

[11] J. A. MONTGOMERY, "New Sources of Knowledge," *R.R.*, p. 22.

The final description is that of a *bōlēs* of sycamores. [1] This word also lacks exact definition. It seems clearly to be related to the semitic word for fig. [2] We might create a word in English for a literal translation: "a *figger* of sycamores." This type of tree bears a small fruit which is processed and eaten throughout the East. [4] Various Greek translations have one who "scratches" [3] or "marks" [5] sycamores, while one lists him as an "owner" [6] of sycamores. Whether Amos is here described as a simple worker [7] or as a substantial owner [8] is not clear. We can only know he had a second occupation in which he had something to do with sycamore-figs.

But there is a further problem about this designation. Since such sycamores appear not to grow at such an altitude as that at Tekoa, [9] this work must have taken Amos either over into the Jordan valley or into the southern *Shephelah* of Judah. [10] Amos was, then, not only a substantial citizen of Tekoa, but one who had business interests elsewhere which caused him to travel about at least as far as the borders of Judah. [11]

For those influences which shaped his basic character and religious outlook, we must look, then, to this rural Judaean village and the broadening influences of travel, keeping in mind that we have no reason to assume that Jerusalem [12] itself played any direct role.

The prophecies of Amos give evidence of certain basic convic-

---

[1] Amos vii 14. Can it be that both these words have "sycamores" for an object? "But I am a keeper and figger of sycamores."

[2] A *hapaxlegomenon*. Similar words in Arabic and Ethiopic mean "fig", while *nbs* in Egyptian means "sycamore fig."

[3] H. N. and Alma L. Moldenke, *Plants of the Bible*, (Waltham, Mass., 1952), pp. 106-108; Cripps, *op. cit.*, p. 235; N. H. Snaith, *op. cit.*, pp. 126-7; E. W. Heaton, *Everyday Life in Old Testament Times* (London, 1956), p. 111; G. E. Wright, *Biblical Archeology* (Philadelphia, 1957), p. 183.

[4] κνίζων—supported by Theodor of Mopsuestia and Theodoret of Cyprus.

[5] Theotocion: χαράσσων; Aquila: ἐρευνών, searcher, examiner.

[6] Symmachus: ἔχων.

[7] S. R. Driver, *Joel and Amos*: *C.B.*, p. 207, "a dresser;" W. R. Smith, *op. cit.*, p. 396, "A splitter of sycamore figs;" Köhler, *op. cit.*, p. 130, "a nipper of sycamore figs;" J. Hempel, *Die althebräische Literatur und ihr hellenistisch-jüdisches Nachleben* (Potsdam, 1930), pp. 127-8.

[8] Würthwein, "Amos Studien," *Z.A.W.* LXII (1950), p. 22: "Sycamoren-züchter", a sycamore-planter.

[9] Cf. Moldenke and others.

[10] Cf. Moldenke, Cripps, and others.

[11] Cripps, *op. cit.*, p. 12; opposed to Hempel, *op. cit.*, p. 128.

[12] E. Würthwein, *Die 'am hā'ārætz im Alten Testament* (Stuttgart, 1936) has shown that one must make a clear distinction between ideas and practices of the two. Cf. R. Meyer, *Judaica* III (1947), p. 169 ff.

tions. [1] Amos had no doubt that Jahweh was Lord and Master [2] of all he surveyed: heaven and earth, [4] man's history and destiny. [3] In addition he believed in Jahweh's election of Israel which was ethically conditioned. [5] Neither of these convictions was new. [6] Both belonged to the basic structure of Jahwistic faith. [7] They were his heritage, not the product of his ministry. [8]

A further heritage of faith which one might expect in Amos was his belief in the election of the Davidic house. [9] The particular character of Amos' task eliminated direct reference to this from the body of his message. [10] Only as he drew his ministry to a close, as he framed his message of judgement within the greater plan of God, did he draw on this element of his heritage for hope that Jahweh would yet fulfill the promise of election [11].

B. AMOS' RELIGIOUS EXPERIENCE

One cannot trace the accounts of religious experience in Amos further back than his call to prophetic service. [12] Even this call is presented in one terse statement: "Jahweh *took* me from following the flock when he said to me, 'Go! *Be a prophet* (prophesy) to my people Israel." [13]

What kind of experience is it that is reflected here? Can we classify

---

[1] V. MAAG, *Text, Wortschatz und Begriffswelt des Buches Amos* (Leiden, 1951), p. 235 ff. has an excellent analysis of Amos' theology.

[2] Cf. *ib.*, pp. 118-119 for a description of Amos' use of "Lord" and "Lord of Hosts."

[3] Amos ii 13; iv 6-7; vii 4; viii 9; ix 2.

[4] Amos i 3 ff.; ix 7.

[5] Amos ii 10; iii 1-2; v 24-25; ix 7, 15.

[6] Cf. particularly the J sections of Exodus.

[7] W. F. ALBRIGHT, *From the Stone Age to Christianity* (2nd ed., Baltimore, 1946), p. 239.

[8] MAAG, *op. cit.*, p. 239 f.; PORTEOUS, *op. cit.*, p. 220.

[9] Cf. II Sam. vii.

[10] He was specifically called to prophesy to Israel according to Amos vii 15.

[11] Amos ix 11.

[12] I. P. SEIERSTAD, *Die Offenbarungserlebnisse der Propheten Amos, Jesaja und Jeremia* (Oslo, 1946), p. 41, has a full bibliography of works on the call of Amos to that date; Cf. also V. HERNTRICH, "Das Berufungsbewusstsein des Amos," *Christentum und Wissenschaft* (1933), p. 161 ff.; J. HEMPEL, "Berufung und Bekehrung", *Festschrift Beer* (1935), p. 41 f.; S. MOWINCKEL, "Die Offenbarungserlebnisse der Propheten Amos, Jesaya und Jeremia," *N.T.T.* XLIX (1948), pp. 120-128.

[13] JEPSON, *op. cit.*, p. 171; A. R. JOHNSON, *The One and the Many in the Israelitic Concept of God* (Cardiff, 1942), p. 36 ff.; ROWLEY, *op. cit.*, p. 112 ff.; WÜRTHWEIN, *Z.A.W.* CXII (1950), p. 24 ff.

it as one of prophetic ecstasy?[1] During the past half century the scholars have battled over that point.[2] Yet even today it is difficult to adequately define prophetic ecstasy.[3]

In regard to Amos, a point of departure may be taken from the word *lāqáḥ*—"Jahweh *took* me."[4] Whatever else the expression may mean, it certainly reflects the prophet's consciousness of direction by a higher will.[5] In a very personal way Jahweh demonstrated his rule over Amos in laying his hand upon him, in claiming him as a particular tool for his purpose. Amos' conviction of the overall Lordship of Jahweh took a practical and personal turn. He felt himself "possessed". He knew himself to be controlled from without. His will was given over to another.

That which Jahweh commands him to do is to "Go! Be a prophet!"[6] The latter word has the same root as the noun *nābī'*, prophet. The verb is a reflexive form, evidently built upon the noun, a denominative verb, meaning simply "be or act the prophet." He was to be a prophet to (אֶל) Israel. There was no hint here of what message he should bring. It was sufficient that Jahweh had taken control of him and commanded him to be a prophet.

From this verse alone one would gather that Amos' position is clear beyond question. But that is far from the case. In just the previous verse Amos had protested vehemently: "I (am) no *nābī'* nor a *bĕn nābī'*!"[7] How are we to understand these two apparently contradictory sentences?

First we must note the context.[8] Amaziah, the priest of Bethel, had just counseled Amos to flee from Bethel because it had become necessary to warn the king that his words were bordering upon

---

[1] K. CRAMER, *Amos* (Stuttgart, 1930), p. 21; MEEK, *op. cit.*, p. 177; J. RIDDERBOS, *Profetie en Ekstase* (Aalten, 1941).

[2] E. A. LESLIE, *Old Testament Religion* (New York, 1946), p. 115.

[3] ROWLEY, *op. cit.*, p. 91 ff.; SEIERSTAD, *op. cit.*, p. 156 ff.; LINDBLOM, *B.F.*, p. 325 ff.; SNAITH, *R.R.*, p. 225.

[4] Cf. Ez. iii 14.

[5] Cf. L. H. BROCKINGTON, "The Lord Showed Me, The Correlation of Natural and Spiritual in Prophetic Experience," *S.H.R.*, pp. 33-34.

[6] This is not as decisive as it may sound. Recent scholars have been asking. What is a *nābī'*? and: Were the great prophets *nĕbī'īm*? Cf. I. HYLANDER, "War Jesaja Nabi?" *Le Monde Oriental* XXV (1931), p. 53 ff.

[7] H. H. ROWLEY, "Was Amos a Nabi?" *Festschrift Otto Eissfeldt* (Halle, 1947), pp. 191-198; A. VAN HOONACKER, "Le sens de la protestation d'Amos VII 14-15," *Ephemerides Theologicae Lovanienses* XVIII (1941), pp. 65-67.

[8] Amos vii 10-17.

C. AMOS' FUNCTIONS AS A PROPHET

The terse recital of his call leaves the reader to assume that Amos obeyed, going to Israel and serving as a prophet there. What did that mean for Amos? As a prophet what was his function and activity? The product of his prophetic activity fills his book.[1] His "words" or messages[2] are evidence that he had to speak for God.[3] The oft-repeated phrases "Thus saith Jahweh"[4] and "expression of Jahweh"[5] are reminders that he was God's messenger or mouthpiece to Israel. He represented God's will to the people through his messages.

Amos' words were formulated with a freshness and originality which arrested attention and authenticated his expression.[6] But the basic forms in which the messages were presented were not new.[7] In them the patterns devised through generations of prophetic activity were adapted as vehicles of God's word to Israel. The poetic meter and style may be classed with the most vigorous and perfect in Hebrew literature;[8] yet it is a mastery of accepted style, not an innovation.[9]

In these words are to be found predictions of history's course[10]

---

[1] The authenticity of Amos' work is generally accepted. Cf. McCullough *J.B.L.* LXXII (1953), p. 247. It is not clear that Amos "wrote" his book. But however the process of recording and transmitting it, most scholars with the exception of the sceptical scandinavian oral-traditionists and a few like R. E. Wolfe, *Meet Amos & Hosea* (N.Y., 1945, p. XVII.) agree on the authentic record of Amos activity. Minor exceptions are to be noted: ii 4-5 and v 13 are generally viewed as later insertions in the text. Some of the foreign prophecies have been contested, but there is no unanimity of opinion there. And the messages of hope (ix 11-15) have today's scholars fairly evenly divided in their views.

[2] Cf. Ludwig Köhler's classification of them as "Botensprüche," *Deutero-jesaja Stilkritisch Untersucht* (*B.Z.A.W.* 37, Giessen, 1923), p. 102; Hempel, *op. cit.*, p. 128.

[3] The observation concerning prophecy generally in n. 6, p. 2 is essentially correct, but it does not eliminate the prophet's use of prediction and other forms in presenting his prohecy. Note A. Bentzen's "The Ritual Background of Amos i 2-ii 16," *O.T.S.* VIII (1950), p. 89 findings that Amos has used old forms for his prophecy. Also M. A. Beek, "The Religious Background of Amos ii 6-8," *O.T.S.* V (1948), p.p 132-141.

[4] Amos i 3, 6, 9, 11, 13; ii 1, 4, 6; iii 12; v 3, 4, 16; vii 17.

[5] Amos i 5, 8, 15; ii 3, 11, 16; iii 13, 15; iv 3, 5, 6, 8, 9, 10, 11; v 17, 27; vii 8. 14; viii 3, 9, 11; ix 7, 8, 12.

[6] Hempel, *op. cit.*, p. 129.

[7] Brockington, *op. cit.*, p. 38.

[8] Hempel, *op. cit.*

[9] Cramer, *op. cit.*, p. 215.

[10] H. C. Ackerman, *A.T.R.* IV (1921-22), p. 116; H. Gunkel, *Exp.* 9th ser. (1924), p. 433; A. Guillaume, *op. cit.*, p. 111.

and penetrating analyses of contemporary religious and social scenes. [1] But Amos never allowed these to become ends in themselves. Both were set within the framework of God's demand for righteousness [2] and his plea for the people to repent. [3] These words were not spoken in answer to people's questions to the itinerant seer. [4] They were proclaimed because the prophet knew that God uttered them. [5] They were voiced within the definite religious setting of Israel's election and God's requirements. [6] Where would that be? Nowhere so clearly and surely as at the New Year's festival [7] (later Feast of Tabernacles) in one of the great sanctuaries. [8] There the great ceremonial occasion reminded all of the covenant and the wonderful election which it promised. [9] There, too, the reading of the law [10]

---

[1] E. DOBSCHUTZ, "Interpretation," *Encyclopedia of Religion and Ethics* VII (London, 1914), p. 395: "Its (exegesis') highest merit consists, not in originality, but in the sureness with which the right thing is seized." Amos had this gift of surely grasping the right thing. Cf. M. F. UNGER, *Israel and the Aramaens of Damascus* (London, 1957), p. 94.

[2] MEEK, *op. cit.*, p. 178, "It is our contention that they (the classical prophets) were a revival of the *nābī'* type of prophet in his original form as champion of Yahweh."

[3] Amos v 4-6, 14-15.

[4] As might often have been the case in earlier prophecy.

[5] WÜRTHWEIN, *op. cit.*, p. 39: "Amos jedenfalls, . . . empfindet keinen Gegensatz zwischen seinem Nabitum und seiner Unheilsverkündigung, ist er doch beides—nur deshalb—weil Jahweh jeweils gerufen hat."

[6] Amos ii 10; iii 2; ix 7; and v 14, 24.

[7] H. J. KRAUS, *Gottesdienst in Israel, Studien zur Geschichte des Laubhüttenfestes* (Munich, 1954).

[8] Bethel is most probable in light of Amos vii 1-17. Cf. R. BRINKER, *The Influence of Sanctuaries in Early Israel* (Manchester, 1946); E. NIELSEN, *Shechem* (Copenhagen, 1955), p. 305 ff.

[9] A. WEISER, *Die Psalmen A.T.D.* XIV (Göttingen, 1950), p. 13 ff.; G. VON RAD, *Das Formgeschichtliche Problem des Hexateuchs* (Stuttgart, 1938); W. EICHRODT, *Theologie des Alten Testaments* I (4th ed. Berlin, 1950) has helped to restore the idea of the covenant to its rightful place of importance in the understanding of Old Testament thought and worship. Several recent works deal ably with the Old Testament doctrine of election: K. GALLING, *Die Erwählungstraditionen Israels* (*B.Z.A.W.* 48, Giessen, 1928); H. H. ROWLEY, *The Biblical Doctrine of Election* (London, 1950); T. C. VRIEZEN, *Die Erwählung Israels nach dem Alten Testament* (*A.T.A.N.T.* 24, Zürich, 1953).

[10] A. ALT, *Die Ursprünge des israelitischen Rechts* (1934): reprinted in *K.S.* I, pp. 278-332; M. NOTH, *Die Gesetze im Pentateuch. Ihre Voraussetzungen und ihr Sinn* (Halle, 1940). G. ÖSTBORN, *Tora in the Old Testament* (Lund, 1945) and *Cult and Canon* (Uppsala, 1950). Strangely enough, in this latter work ÖSTBORN in his anxiety to stress the narrative and dramatic nature of canonical material seems to omit a description of the place of law in ritual altogether. Cf. also R. BACH, "Gottesrecht u. weltliches Recht in der Verkündigung des Propheten Amos," *Festschrift für Günther Dehn* (ed. W. Schneemelcher, Neukirchen, 1957), pp. 34-48.

should have been emphasized, [1] though records of the times would indicate that this was much neglected. There Amos spoke to gathered throngs and spoiled many a festive mood through his unabashed denunciation of evil [2] and call to repentance. [3] There the complacent assurance of many an Israelite merchant and his opulent consort were shaken by his assured predictions of judgement. [4] But the records of Amos' ministry show other sides of his life as a prophet as well. They record a series of great experiences with God. [5] It lies beyond our powers to exactly analyse the psychic or psychological form of these experiences. [6] Each account tells of a vision, whether a natural object which drew his attention or whether completely psychic and independent of his surroundings is unclear. [7] In each one God "shows" [8] him an object [9] or a scene. [10] Each in turn is interpreted [11] as a judgement of God. [12]

---

[1] WÜRTHWEIN, op. cit. speaks of Amos' relations to the Law, and of law in the cult, but he fails to show the setting of the law in the sanctuary where Amos was. This still remains to be shown.

[2] Amos ii 6-8; v 10-12; vi 1-7.

[3] Amos v 4-6, 14.

[4] Amos iv 1-3.

[5] Amos vii 1-9; viii 1-3; ix 1.

[6] Attempts like OBBINK's "Forms of Prophetism," *H.U.C.A.* XIV (1939), pp. 23-28 leave the impression of being more clever than convincing. He certainly oversimplifies the relation of the great prophets to the "nĕbî'îm." If his test of prophecy ("whether they turn the people from evil") were applied, which prophet could pass? Jer. xxiii 22 does not describe results, but rather the aims of prophecy.

[7] Cf. M. SISTER, "Die Typen der prophetischen Visionen in der Bibel," *M.G.W.J.* LXXVIII (1934), pp. 399-430.

[8] Amos vii 1, 4, 6; viii 1. The accounts stress that the initiative belongs to God.

[9] Amos vii 1 (locusts); vii 7 (a plumbline). But it should be noticed that in each God is pictured as forming, or holding, or acting with the object seen. Only in Amos viii 1 does the object stand alone.

[10] Amos vii 4 presents a scene which is dominated by cultic motifs. The final vision (ix 1ff.) also presents a scene in which cult patterns and prophetic fulfillment seem mixed together.

[11] WÜRTHWEIN, op. cit., p. 41 has noted that prophecy of judgement is composed of two elements: the irrational announcement of judgement and the rational justification of it. GRESSMANN, op. cit., p. 93 has said something of the same thing in contending that before Amos prophets only had to predict the future on the basis of God's word given to them. Beginning with Amos, they sought to understand and explain these predictions as growing from an inner necessity. S. MOWINCKEL, "Ecstatic Experience and Rational Elaboration in Old Testament Prophecy," *A.O.* XIII (1934-5), pp. 264-291.

[12] To the references listed in note 1, p. 4 above should be added H. W. WOLF, "Die Begründungen der prophetischen Heils- und Unheilssprüche," *Z.A.W.* LII (1934), pp. 1-21.

When the visions are understood as formative experiences [1] following the prophet's call [2] and extending throughout his ministry, [3] they are seen to mark chapters in his development. Each one characterized a period in the formation of the prophet's understanding of his mission and message. [4] In these experiences God led Amos to "see" his interpretation of the times. "Seeing" preceded[5] and made possible prophetic speech.

But the visions picture another essential prophetic function. It is that of intercession. [6] Twice Amos pleads successfully with Jahweh on behalf of Israel. [7]

The prophetic functions, [8] then, begin in "seeing" God's intention for the people. When this is good, [9] the prophet has only to proclaim it, thereby comforting the people [11] and also actually helping it to come to pass. [11] But if this vision is one of judgement instead of salvation, [12]

---

[1] See the argument of ch. II, "Vision and Oracle," on this point.

[2] To be distinguished from the views of Weiser that they led up to his call.

[3] Even beyond his Bethel experience to chapters 8 and 9.

[4] WATTS, "The Origin of the Book of Amos," *Ex. T.* LXVI (1955), pp. 109-112.

[5] Cf. S. MOWINCKEL, "The Spirit and the Word in the Pre-exilic Reforming Prophets," *J.B.L.* LIII (1934), pp. 199-227.

[6] The prophetic function of intercession has recently been stressed by WÜRTHWEIN, *op. cit.*, p. 26 f.; JOHNSON, *The Cultic Prophet*; Cf. also VON RAD, "Falsche Propheten," *Z.A.H.* CI (1933), p. 114; J. HEMPEL, *Gott und Mensch im Alten Testament* (2nd. ed., Stuttgart, 1936), p. 126ff.; P. A. H. DE BOER, *De Voorbede in Het Oude Testament* (*O.T.S.* III, Leiden, 1943), pp. 157-161; A. S. HERBERT, "The Prophet as Intercessor," *Baptist Quarterly* XIII (April, 1949), pp. 76-80; F. HESSE, *Die Fürbitte im Alten Testament* (Erlangen, 1949).

[7] Amos vii 2, 4.

[8] In addition to the works noted in p. 3, n. 5 and p. 4, n. 1, cf. H. JUNKER, *Prophet und Seher in Israel* (Trier, 1927); A. R. JOHNSON, "The Prophet in Israelite Worship," *Ex. T.* XLVII (1938), pp. 312-319.

[9] Surely von RAD (*op. cit.*, p. 110ff.) is oversimplifying in saying that cult prophets are exclusively prophets of salvation while writing prophets bring messages of judgement. JOHNSON (*op. cit.*) also speaks about cult prophets as necessarily prophets of salvation and peace. WÜRTHWEIN (*op. cit.*, p. 26) concurs in saying their task was to uphold the šālôm of king and people.

[10] Cf. Isaiah xl 1. Cf. also H. W. HERZBERG, "Die prophetische Botschaft vom Heil und die alttestamentliche Theologie," *N.K.Z.* (1932), pp. 513-34.

[11] O. GRETHER, *Name u. Wort Gottes im Alten Testament* (*B.Z.A.W.* 64, Giessen, 1934), p. 103; G. FOHRER, *Die symbolischen Handlungen der Propheten* (*A.T.A.N.T.* 25, Zürich, 1953).

[12] WÜRTHWEIN, *op. cit.*, while recognizing the basic positive function of the prophets, notes that a special call of God has given an opposite message to prophets like Isaiah, Jeremiah, and Ezekiel. JOHNSON, *op. cit.*, by listing intercession as one of the functions of the prophet has recognized the possibility of such a vision of judgement.

one of curse instead of blessing, (and such a possibility must be open where there is any true prediction) what is that prophet's function then? First notice that it does *not* necessarily entail a pronouncement which makes its fulfillment inevitable. [1] The prophet may utter the dire tidings in terms of a call to repentance thus hoping to turn aside this consequence of sin. [2] And he may intercede with God on their behalf. [3]

These are functions which belonged to any true *nābī'* in Israel. [4] They are functions which Amos fulfilled. But if the people did not repent, [5] and if God's patience was at an end, [6] what then? Then the prophet could only invoke final judgement with the same effect as that in pronouncing blessing. [7] Was Amos the first who had to do this? By no means. [8] But never before had it been necessary thus to officiate at the funeral of a whole people. [9] Always before it had been the end of a regime, [10] or punishment of a small part, [11] or for a limited time. [12] But the function was here the same. Only in degree was Amos different.

One negative statement needs to be added in this discussion of prophetic function. Amos was accused of inciting revolt and assassination, [13] and this had often been a function of prophetic pronounce-

---

[1] Note the judgements pictured in Amos vii 1-6 which effective intercession turned aside.

[2] Amos v 4-7, 14-15.

[3] As indeed Amos does in vii 2 and 5.

[4] If it be conceded that a prediction of this type of judgement must precede intercession, all the sources cited in note 6, p. 16 would support this.

[5] Amos ii 11-12; iv 6-11; Isaiah vi 9-10; Jer. i 19; Ez. iii 7.

[6] Amos iv 12; vii 7-9.

[7] Cf. Note 11, p. 16. This gives his words the effect of a curse instead of a blessing.

[8] Surely a healthy critical analysis of the sources would not write off the consistent presentation of prophecies of judgement and censure as inventions of later writers. Cf. I Sam. xv 23; II Sam. xii 10-11; xxiv 13; I Kings xiv 4-13; xvii 1; xix 15-16; xxii 17-23 and 28.

[9] Here Israel: at least the northern kingdom. A later parallel is to be found in the prophecies of Jeremiah and Ezekiel. Cf. W. ZIMMERLI, *Erkenntnis Gottes nach dem Buche Ezechiel* (*A.T.A.N.T.* 27, Zürich, 1954), pp. 70-71.

[10] As Ahijah's prophecy concerning Jeroboam: I Kings xiv 4-13, or Elijah-Elisha concerning Ahab: II Kings ix 1-3.

[11] Judges xx 18 does not specifically speak of prophetic activity, but it does present a situation in which the people are directed by oracular means (whether prophetic or priestly) in carrying out judgement against a part of itself. The setting is clearly one in which a prophecy of judgement would be at home.

[12] As Elijah's announcement of a drought: I Kings xvii 1.

[13] Amos vii 10-11.

ments. [1] But there is no evidence that Amos was in any sense a political revolutionary. [2] At that point he saw God moving on the great canvas of history to accomplish his judgement. What time had he for palace intrigues?

D. AMOS' RELATION TO THE CULT

Any discussion on this point has to be based, in the very nature of the case, on circumstantial evidence. If the interpretation of Amos vii 14 given above is correct, then it is not permissible to introduce it as evidence against his participation in cult activity. [3]

First it should be noted that Amos seemed to appear regularly at the sanctuaries. [4] He seems certainly to have prophesied in Samaria [5] and Bethel. [6] He was known to Amaziah by name. And his frequent mention of Gilgal, [7] Carmel, [8] and others [9] may imply his having participated in festival occasions [10] there also.

The second evidence may be drawn from his intimate acquaintance with cult functions [11] and abuses [12] which is reflected in his messages.

---

[1] Ahijah, Elisha, and many others. Cf. J. MORGENSTERN, "Amos Studies III, The Historical Antecedents of Amos' Prophecy," *H.U.C.A.* XV (1940), pp. 59-304; A. NEHER, *Amos* (Paris, 1950), pp. 173-210.

[2] Morgenstern, *op. cit.*, p. 289.

[3] ROWLEY, "Was Amos a *Nabi*?" *op. cit.*, pp. 191 ff. records an adequate bibliography of those using this argument. To these might be added the reference, W. S. McCULLOUGH, "Some Suggestions about Amos," *J.B.L.* LXXII (1953), p. 251.

[4] Recent works have tended to show a distinct relation between prophecy and cult: MOWINCKEL, *P.S.* III; PEDERSEN, *Israel I-II*, p. 115; I. ENGNELL, *Gamla Testamentet* (Stockholm, 1945), p. 152 ff.; Id., "Amos," *S.B.U.* I (1948), cols. 59-61; Id. "Profeter," *S.B.U.* II (1952), cols. 727-775; HALDAR, *op. cit.*, p. 112.

[5] Amos iii 9-12; iv 1-3; vi 1; viii 14.

[6] Amos iii 14; iv 4; vii 10-17.

[7] Amos iv 4; v 5.

[8] Amos i 2; ix 3.

[9] Beersheba (v 5; viii 14); Dan (viii 14).

[10] Festivals are the normal occasions on which one makes a pilgrimage to these places. Cf. A. ALT, "Die Wallfahrt von Sichem nach BETHEL, *K.S.* I, pp. 79-88; C. A. KELLER, "Die Wallfahrt von Sichem nach Bethel," *Schweizerisches Kirchenblatt für die reformierte Schweiz* (1955-11).

[11] With no attempt to list allusions to cult motifs, the following are still quite clear: Amos i 2; ii 14; iv 4-5; v 5; v 21-23, 25; viii 10. McCULLOUGH, *op. cit.*, p. 251 notes this, but denies cult tradition. He would see Amos rather in the tradition of Moses, Nathan, Elijah. However, cf. note 9, p. 19 and KAPELRUD, *op. cit.*, p. 68 ff.

[12] Amos ii 7-8 and 12; v 26; vii 9; viii 14. Cf. F. B. SHOOT, *The Fertility Religions in the Thought of Amos and Micah*, (*Dissertation*: *Univ. of Southern California*, 1951);

Amos was related to cult:
1. He mentions cultic centers
2. Familiar with cult functions & abuses
3. Had to be related

These could best be explained if his service as a prophet had given him ample opportunity to observe these abuses.

But these alone are not sufficient proof unless a third observation is justified. We have observed that Amos described his call as one to become a prophet (*nābī'*) [1] to Israel. Was it possible to be a prophet and fulfill a prophet's functions without being related to the cult in some way? [2]

This question touches on a sore point and turns upon one's understanding of what is meant by cult prophecy. [3] If the term is taken to indicate participation in cult divination or similar rites, [4] then one must answer that O.T. prophecy appears only incidentally and occasionally to be related to any such activity. [5] Such a picture is as far from that in Amos as can be. [6] But is this an accurate picture of Israelitic cult prophecy?

The picture of the prophets and bands of prophets in the O.T. seems to center much more in functions connected with the Jahwistic traditions of the people. [7] He, alongside the priest, helped preserve the right relations within the covenant. [8] He, especially, was Jahweh's spokesman, [9] proclaiming his

---

M. LEAHY, "The Popular Idea of God in Amos," *Irish Theological Quarterly* XXII (1955), pp. 68-73; C. Gant, "Religious Worship in the Book of Amos," *Melita Theologica* III (1950), pp. 75-93, IV (1951), pp. 34-48.

[1] Amos vii 15 has an imperative verbal form of this root which has been variously translated, "prophesy," "be a prophet," and "act as a prophet."

[2] WÜRTHWEIN, *op. cit.*, p. 26 has insisted that men were called to the prophetic office. Cf. also references in note 175 and questions raised by LINDBLOM, *B.F.*, p. 327 ff.

[3] The range of opinions runs from that of ecstatic members of roving prophetic bands in the Canaanite pattern, through JOHNSON's picture (*op. cit.*) of "Heilspropheten" who, proved liars by the exile, were then degraded to the position of singers in the second temple only to finally disappear, to those who equate cultic and classical prophecy.

[4] Cf. HALDAR, *op. cit.* and BIČ, *op. cit.*

[5] J. PEDERSEN, *Israel III-IV* (Copenhagen, 1940), p. 125.

[6] There seems no single instance in which a word in Amos may be understood as even giving answer to a query put to him by one seeking an oracle. Here without exception the initiative is with God who then moves his prophet to speak.

[7] MEEK, *op. cit.*; G. H. DAVIES, "The Yahwistic Tradition in the Eighth Century Prophets," *S.O.T.P.*, pp. 37-51.

[8] PEDERSEN, *op. cit.*, p. 107; WÜRTHWEIN, *op. cit.*; JOHNSON, *op. cit.*

[9] H. J. KRAUS, *op. cit.*, p. 110 ff. argues that the old celebration of the autumn festival of Jahweh required one to officiate as the mediator of the Covenant. This was simultaneously an office and "charisma," Moses and Samuel serving as fitting examples. Their task was to speak God's will to the people. It is their function to speak the apodictic laws of the covenant. As officials of the cult

will [1] and predicting the future [2] accordingly. He was a preacher of repentance [3] within the covenant and in view of the covenant's requirements. [4] He was likewise an intercessor for his people. [5] These functions were served in relation to Jahwistic ritual and festival. [6] If any such thing, as Jahwistic cult prophecy, existed (and the evidence [7] is accumulating that it did exist), these were the functions it served in the cult. As we have seen above, Amos performed exactly these tasks.

But Amos appeared to be semi-independent of group discipline and life. [8] He was much more like Elijah [9] than Elisha. [10] But we must also ask whether the *běně něbî'îm* were full-time prophets? Were they employed at the sanctuaries the year round? [11] We simply do not know. [12] Were all of them accomplished practicing seers and preachers? [13] Of this we are also ignorant.

---

they repeat the traditional conditions of the Covenant. As called and gifted spokesman for God, they spoke pertinent new messages to the people in this capacity as they were inspired. The king came to fill the official side of this function, but it was left to the prophets to continue the "charismatic" functions of this covenant mediator. "Die 'Schriftpropheten' sind ihrem innersten Wesen nach charismatische Rechtssprecher . . ."

[1] Hence the typical expression: "Hear the word of the Lord." Hence also the typical designation of sin as "disobedience, rebellion, etc."

[2] The conditional character of so many predictions finds its explanation here.

[3] Cf. Is. i 12-20; Ez. xviii and many others.

[4] Particularly the requirements set forth in apodictic law in contrast to those for ritual actions.

[5] KRAUS, *op. cit.*, p. 117.

[6] If KRAUS' method may be followed, especially in covenant ritual related to the New Year's festival.

[7] EISSFELDT, *op. cit.*, p. 119.

[8] There is no sign of any such affiliation; even Amaziah could address him as an individual with no indication that his fate involved any others related to him. GRESSMANN, *Messias*, p. 77 "Die grossen Propheten sind äusserlich und innerlich unabhängig."

[9] In all his appearance except his journey across Jordan he stands quite alone. Even on that last journey (II Kings ii) Elisha always acts as intermediary between Elijah and the groups of prophets who greet them.

[10] Cf. II Kings ii 15-18; iv 1; 38; and many other references to his relations to the *běně nebî'im*.

[11] The freedom of movement of such men as Elijah and Elisha would seem to indicate a negative answer. Yet the groups of prophets who met Elisha at various places seem to have been at home in those areas, with no indication that they traveled about.

[12] To assume such a large number of permanent cult personnel in each local sanctuary is without any stronger foundation than that there were no official servants of the worshipping places.

[13] Would, for instance, Gehazi, Elisha's servant, be counted as one of the *běně nebî'im*?

Until these gaps in our knowledge of Israel's prophetic practice are satisfactorily filled, we are left to assume that Amos followed his calling, becoming a *nābī*', and serving under God's direction like any other faithful prophet at those occasions and in those places where they generally served. [1]

So far we have seen how in form, experience, and institutional connection Amos' ministry fitted a pattern well-known in Israelitic prophecy. *Nabiism* was a complex and manifold institution which could include quite opposite types such as Elijah and Elisha yet recognize in each of them the marks of the true prophet. [2]

Divergence from basic Jahwistic theology [3] and practice or the substitution of auto-suggestion for true inspiration [4] produced examples worthy only of the designation "false prophet." [5] But variations among true prophets were often caused simply by differences in personality. Whether examples are before or after Amos, the result is the same. [6] Jahweh's possession of the prophet does not eliminate his distinctive personal qualities. [7] Further differences were dictated by the historical settings [8] and the requirements of the hour. [9] The message of the great quartet of 8th century prophets could not have been given a century earlier, for truly their "hour had not yet come." But one must not lose sight of that which produced the truly distinctive element in· each prophet: that incomprehensible and unexplainable "call" and direction by his God. [10]

In spite of all these differences, there was a core of similarity in all

---

[1] K. ROUBOS, *Profetie en Cultus in Israel* (Wageningen, 1956), pp. 116 and 121.

[2] ROWLEY, *Prophecy and Religion in Ancient China and Israel* (London, 1956), p. 120—"The prophets of Israel desired to make the ritual more meaningful, not merely more correct."

[3] Like Jezebel's *Ba'al* prophets. BROCKINGTON, *S.H.R.*, p. 41-42.

[4] The basic test of prophecy in fulfillment of prediction is designed to show up this error: Dt. xviii 20-22. It is at this point that most of those prophets who opposed the classical prophets stand indicted. Cf. W. STAERK, "Das Wahrheitskriterium der alttestamentlichen Prophetie," *Z.S.T.* (1928), p. 76 ff.

[5] Cf. note 3, p. 4 above.

[6] Whether one contrast Elijah-Elisha or Jeremiah-Ezekiel-Dt. Isaiah, the glaring differences in personality, style, and theology are apparent.

[7] PORTEOUS, *R.R.*, p. 246; BROCKINGTON, *op. cit.*, p. 35; ROWLEY, *S.L.*, p. 120.

[8] The contribution which 19th and 20th century critical study has made to an understanding of the historical background and relevance of the prophets should certainly not be abandoned now.

[9] Note this supreme quality of revelance which only can account for a chapter like xviii in Ezekiel.

[10] Cf. H. W. ROBINSON, *Redemption* and *Revelation* (Oxford, 1942), p. 143;J. P. HYATT, *Prophetic Religion* (N.Y., 1947), p. 17.

true prophecy. The likenesses centered in a basically similar theology.[1] Each displayed fundamental convictions related to Jahweh's covenant with Israel. [2] Their "ecstasies" never took them outside of this basic environment of faith, but rather helped them develop and "see" inferences drawn from these convictions. [3] Similarity is furthered through the basic religious and social institution [4] to which the prophets belonged. The bands gave continuity to the movement and are probably responsible for the preservation of the "words", "visions", and biographies of the prophets. But a further unity may be observed in the stream of Israel's prophecy indicated by signs that these prophets served God's purpose in relation to his covenant people and through them served all humanity.

E.   AMOS' MESSAGE

Amos' call did not define his message. [5] It determined only his authority, [6] his function, [7] and his field of activity. [8] On the other hand, the visions were recorded to demonstrate how his distinctive message was formed [9] and to justify such a drastic prophecy. [10] In them a distinct development may be traced both in regard to the prophet's understanding and to the message given to him. [11] They also reflect the progressive fixation of God's intentions in light of the

---

[1] A. C. Welch, *Prophet and Priest in Old Israel* (Oxford, 1936), p. 68.

[2] CRAMER, *op. cit.*, p. 214-15.

[3] H. D. F. SPARKS, "The Witness of the Prophets to Hebrew Tradition," *J.T.S.* L (1949), pp. 129-141; G. H. DAVIES, *op. cit.*, pp. 37-51; G. G. HARROP, *Tradition and Dissent in the Eighth-Century Prophets and Jeremiah* (diss. Univ. of Chicago, 1951).

[4] In the first instance, Israel of the Covenant, but in a more restricted sense the sanctuaries and their prophets.

[5] WÜRTHWEIN, *op. cit.*, p. 28 f. Amos vii 15, "Go be a prophet to my people Israel." The change of בקר to נקד as Weiser suggests (p. 261), is arbitrary. Cf. SCHMIDT and KÖHLER.

[6] Amos vii 16, "Therefore, hear the word of Jahweh."

[7] "Be a prophet."

[8] Israel (specifically, Northern Israel, but the implication of "All Israel" is not lacking).

[9] See chap. II.

[10] WÜRTHWEIN, *op. cit.*, p. 35. TH. C. VRIEZEN, "Prophecy and Eschatology," *S.V.T.* I (1953), p. 204, n. 3 attributes Amos' radical prophecy to his call.

[11] These two must be thought of neither as identical nor as having nothing to do with each other. Rather one should probably understand a constant interaction between them which makes possible application and interpretation of the message.

people's response to previous messages. [1] Amos was intensely aware of this interrelation of initiative and response as it affected God's attitude toward Israel. [2]

The first account tells of a natural catastrophe which swept through Israel, a plague of locusts. [3] The vision was not momentary. Amos observed it in its beginnings, [4] saw its implications as a judgement of God, [5] but did not make his plea for forgiveness until its destructive work was done. [6] How is this lapse of time to be explained? One might explain it psychologically by the capacity of vision or dream · to review a longer period in a moment. But the "vision" seems to recount the prophet's experiences over a considerable time. If the experiences were real, the account telescoped the impressions of a considerable period into a brief report. The prophet's message in this period must have been one warning of God's judgement through the locusts and pleading with the people to repent, [7] a message not uncommon in Old Testament prophecy. [8] The prophet's function was positive: through warning, preaching, and intercession to bring or preserve salvation. [9] But his basic message was judgement even in this first phase.

The second vision [10] centered in the "fire" [11] of Jahweh and the destruction it wrought on ocean depths and dry land. The form of the judgement had changed, but its purpose and message remained essentially the same. Prophetic intercession was able a second time to gain forgiveness. This form of judgement was broader in application, [12] was more expressive of the judgement of a transcendent Lord. [13] It is no surprise to find the motif reflected in Amos'

---

[1] Würthwein, op. cit., p. 30-34 has correctly noted that the increased finality with which Amos prophesied judgement was not due simply to a progression of the prophet's understanding but to a change in Jahweh's own intentions, "ein Wandel in Jahweh selbst."

[2] Amos v 15.

[3] A not uncommon occurrence, perhaps commonly understood as some sort of judgement like that of drought. Cf. Joel i 4.

[4] Amos vii 1 "forming locusts."

[5] This is implied by the succeding intercession.

[6] Amos vii 2, "When they had finished eating the grass of the land".

[7] The period is seen in retrospect in Amos iv 9.

[8] Joel i 4-12; I K. xvii f. (Elijah prophesies a drought).

[9] Even as God's purpose in the "judgement" was the positive one of bringing about repentance as Amos iv 6-11 shows.

[10] Amos vii 4-6.

[11] V. Maag, "Jahwäs Heerscharen," Köhler Festschrift, S.T.U. XX (1950), p. 49.

[12] Its cosmic proportions are emphasized by "the great deep" and "the land".

[13] Cf. Gen. xix 24; Num. xvi 35.

foreign prophecies. [1] Here God does not conquer the nations through the armies of Israel, [2] but wreaks destruction through the direct application of destructive "fire." [3] In this figure a potential destruction of all is possible, [4] but is restrained through the prophet's intercession and Jahweh's mercy. Here, at least, the potential scope of Jahweh's judgement is clearly in view. [5]

The third vision [6] is more specific and definitive. Jahweh's standard was set in the midst of his people. [7] The reason for Jahweh's judgement was all too obvious in the people's disobedience and rebellion. Such a standard served to pin-point the source of Israel's trouble in the court [8] and in the royally sponsored cult. [9] It was their sin and failure which had led Israel to this lamentable state of corruption. But at that point God suspended the normal functions of the covenant relation [10] with their possibilities for intercession, repentance, and forgiveness. [11] The prophet's message could only be a pronouncement of doom on the "sinful kingdom," [12] specifically upon its central organs, the royal house and the royal sanctuaries.

At this point the message of Amos was complete. The final two visions confirmed [13] and in part fulfilled [14] the message of the third, but there was no change affecting Israel's fate.

The visions, then, show us how Amos' message of judgement began as a part of normal prophetic functions. When Amos was

---

[1] Amos i 4, 7, 10, 12, 14; ii 2, 5; and against Joseph in v 6.

[2] As would have been common in the earlier pattern of holy war. Cf. PEDERSEN, *Israel* III-IV, pp. 1-32; von RAD, *Der Heilige Krieg im alten Israel* (*A.T.A.N.T.* 20, Zurich, 1951).

[3] Cf. Lev. x 2 and I Kings xviii 38.

[4] The accomplished destruction of the *Tĕhōm* and the threatened destruction of the land show this all too clearly.

[5] Is this a cultic motif which would indicate that this scope of potential judgement was known in Israel? Or is this something quite new through Amos? Cf. chap. IV.

[6] Amos vii 7-9.

[7] The plumb line's character as a standard for testing is obvious.

[8] Amos vii 9, 10.

[9] Amos vii 9 and iii 14; iv 4; v 21-23.

[10] This is the implication of "I will never pass by them again," and the announcement of judgement directed at the monarchy and sanctuaries. The fourth vision (vii 1-3) with its message, "the end upon my people Israel" confirms this.

[11] Sacrifice also belongs here, although Amos seems to view its validity as already gone (v 22). Of course, this is the reason for no intercession following this vision.

[12] Cf. Amos ix 8.

[13] Amos viii 1-3.

[14] Amos ix 1 ff.

given to see an adverse future, he interpreted it as God's judgement [1] and announced it with a plea for repentance. At the same time he represented the people to God in a plea for forgiveness.

But they show us, further, how Amos was given to see God testing the people in light of the covenant. Refusal to fulfill the conditions of the covenant made it necessary to announce judgement which was not simply chastisement, but destruction. A judgement to which the ordinary provisions of forgiveness within the covenant no longer applied.

Beyond the visions Amos' message took one more step. In wrestling with the implications which his message had in regard to his convictions of Israel's election, [2] he was given to see God's continuation of his covenant with the Davidic house [3] and the assurance that the "end" [4] for the Israel of the ten tribes was not the "end" for the Israel of God. [5] Here he deposited a foundation on which others continued to build. [6]

---

[1] Three forms of judgement appear in Amos. The first, illustrated in the first vision and iv 6-11 is that of chastisement intended to bring about repentence. The second, represented by the second vision and also pictured in ii 13-16 and ch. vii, is of judgement as a kind of ordeal intended to destroy the dross and purify the remnant. And the third is more final: an actual destruction seen in the third vision. This third variety may, of course, be viewed as in actualization in history of the unmitigated effects of the ordeal.

[2] Amos iii 2; ix 7-10.

[3] Amos ix 11.

[4] Amos viii 2.

[5] Many have questioned why Amos did not preach the same judgement against abuses in Judah. McCULLOUGH, op. cit., p. 249 is probably right in speaking of a period of his ministry in Judah (Cf. ch. II), but he is on much weaker ground in asking (p. 250), "How could Amos leave out condemnation of the South, being the kind of man he was?" and concluding that he spoke to "all Israel." GORDIS, "The Composition and Structure of Amos," H.T.R. XXXIII (1940), p. 242 is certainly correct in saying he was neither ignorant of nor indifferent to conditions in Judah. Prophecy is not determined by the character of the prophet, but by the call and inspiration of God. N. SNAITH, The Distinctive Ideas of the Old Testament (Philadelphia, 1946), p. 147 and MAAG, Text Amos, p. 227, n. 10 correctly note that his call limited his activity to Israel. His messages as well as history have shown how valid this call was in stating that the day of doom had dawned for Israel but not yet for Judah. However, SNAITH's conclusion (p. 147) that a message of doom toward the north and one of hope for the south rested on national sentiment lacks support. Not national feeling, but problems of faith and theology raised by this catastrophic judgement in light of God's election and promises force Amos to look for hope toward Judah.

[6] It is to be noted here that Amos preceded Isaiah with both the concept of a remnant (ix 8-10) and that of a Davidic restoration (ix 11-12). An increasing number of critical scholars are coming to recognize these latter verses as authentic: MAAG, op. cit., pp. 247-251.

In announcing dissolution of God's covenant relations with Israel, which involved suspension of other prophetic and priestly functions, [1] Amos was fulfilling the time-honored duty of the *nābīʾ*. [2] His contribution is unique in that the particular message given to him belonged to a uniquely critical point in the history of God's relation to Israel. His inimitable personality and spiritual power would have made him outstanding in any crowd, just as he actually is from the ranks of the *nĕbīʾīm*. His call, his function, his ministry, and his message did not dissolve in the ashes of the dying state to which he ministered, [3] for in spite of his exclusive service to that economy his life and ministry were laid on a much firmer and broader foundation.

---

[1] CRAMER, *op. cit.*, p. 94.

[2] M. BUBER, *The Prophetic Faith* (New York, 1949), p. 110: "Amos did not introduce a new element into Israel's relation to the deity, a relation founded and constituted in another age, but he did set up the exclusiveness of a people in its relation to its God, as to the liberator, leader, and judge of the peoples, lord of righteousness and justice, he set it up under divine demand and chastisement in a manner such as nobody before in man's history so far as we know had achieved . . ." He was "a man given up to the oneness of his God."

[3] Through all our enquiry into the validity of the prophet we are brought back to the fundamental question: Was he of God? Succeeding generations have never failed to render a positive verdict to this ultimate question. Cf. ROWLEY, "Old Testament Prophecy and Recent Study," *op. cit.*, p. 123 ff.; J. WOODS, *The Old Testament in the Church* (London, 1949), p. 25.

CHAPTER TWO

VISION AND ORACLE IN AMOS

In 1929 ARTUR WEISER published the most thorough and searching study of the structure of the Book of Amos which we possess today. [1] He distinguished between two books now incorporated in one : [2] a "Book of Visions" consisting only of the five vision passages, [3] which is the result of Amos' religious experiences in the time before his "call" to be a prophet and which records Amos' earliest utterances, [4] and a "Book of Words." [5]

This work has earned deserved praise for its contribution to the study of prophetic religious experience and its insistence that the message and work of a prophet can only be understood when seen in the light of his "experience of God." [6]

Two others have thought of Amos in terms of two books, but both differ from WEISER and each other on the point of division. [7] I have published my support of the two-book theory arrived at through an analysis of the superscription of Amos. [8] But my description of the books as well as the order of events in the life of

---

[1] *Die Profetie des Amos (B.Z.A.W.* LIII, Giessen, 1929).

[2] *Ibid.*, p. 249; A. WEISER, *Einleitung in das Alte Testament* (2nd. ed., Göttingen, 1949), p. 181-182; A. WEISER, *Das Buch der zwölf Kleinen Propheten I (A.T.D.* XXIV, Göttingen, 1949), pp. 110-113; J. HEMPEL, *Die Althebräische Literatur und Ihr Hellenistisch-Jüdisches Nachleben* (Potsdam, 1930), p. 129; V. MAAG, "Amosbuch," *R.G.G.* I (3rd ed., 1956), cols. 330-331.

[3] WEISER, *Die Propheten Amos*, pp. 249-271; H. GRESSMANN, *Der Messias* (Göttingen, 1929), p. 69 distinguishes two great types of prophecy: Visions and auditions (words).

[4] WEISER, *op. cit.*, pp. 9-77.

[5] *Ibid.*, pp. 272 ff.

[6] *Ibid.*, pp. 1, 250, and others.

[7] J. MORGENSTERN, "Amos Studies I," *H.U.C.A.* XI (1936), pp. 19-140 distinguishes one book composed of the visions, the historical section (vii 10-17) and iii 3-8, 14b, 15 and a second composed of the rest of chapters i-vi. R. GORDIS, "The Composition and Structure of Amos," *H.T.R.* XXXIII (1940), pp. 239-251 writes of one book recording the speeches and events before the encounter at Bethel (i 2-vii 9), a second recording later speeches and visions (viii-ix), with the historical section (vii 10-17) being added to the former before it became joined to the latter. This process is viewed as parallel to that in the Book of Isaiah.

[8] "The Origin of the Book of Amos," *Ex. T.* LXVI (1955), pp. 109-112.

Amos differed from WEISER at several points. It is the purpose of this chapter to explain and support those suggestions.

For all of WEISER's brilliance in analysing Amos, he failed to satisfactorily account for two passages [1] which now separate the third, [2] fourth, [3] and fifth visions [4] from each other. Our investigation will begin with a study of the visions as prophetic literature and then deal with their relation to the biography and "words" of Amos. In this way we may profitably study the relation of these three types of prophetic literature [5] to each other in Amos and gain a conception of the whole book. Behind the literature, however, lay deep experience, as WEISER has shown, [6] and this study should contribute to a better understanding of that experience as well.

A. THE VISIONS OF AMOS

The accounts of Amos' visionary experiences are found in chapters vii-ix of his book. The visions are clearly distinguishable. The first comprises vii 1-3 and the second vii 4-6. The second pair are to be distinguished sharply from the "fragmentary messages" [7] which are attached to them and should be regarded as vii 7-8 and viii 1-2. The fifth vision is decidedly different in form and character and probably should be viewed as including ix 1-4. [8]

---

[1] *Op. cit.*, p. 261 f.: Amos vii 10-17 and viii 14-14; Cf. R. H. PFEIFFER, *Introduction to the Books of the Old Testament* (New York, 1941), p. 579.

[2] Amos vii 7-8 (9).

[3] Amos viii 1-3.

[4] Amos ix 1 ff.

[5] Credit for distinguishing these principal forms of prophetic literature must go to S. MOWINCKEL, *Zur Komposition des Buches Jeremia* (Kristiana, 1914). But also see, J. LINDBLOM, *Die literarische Gattung der prophetischen Literatur*, (*U.U.A.*, Uppsala, 1924), pp. 1-122; id., "The Character of Prophetic Literature," *Ex. T.* LII (1940-41), pp. 126-31; T. H. ROBINSON, *Z.A.W.* XLV (1927); S. MOWINCKEL, *Z.A.W.* XLIX (1931); O. EISSFELDT, "Zur Überlieferungsgeschichte der Prophetenbücher des Alten Testaments," *T.L.Z.* LXXIII (1948), cols. 529-534; H. RINGGREN, "Oral and Written Transmission in the Old Testament," *Studia Theologica* I (1950), p. 34 .; C. R. NORTH, "The Place of Oral Tradition in the Growth of the Old Testament," *Ex. T.* LXI (1949), pp. 292-296; E. VOEGELIN, *Israel and Revelation* (Louisiana State University, 1956), pp. 470-471.

[6] *Op. cit.*, p. 73 ff.; W. RUDOLPH, "Gott und Mensch bei Amos," *Imago Dei, Gustav Krüger Festschrift* (Giessen, 1932), p. 24.

[7] MAAG, *Text Amos*, pp. 47-48.

[8] With CRIPPS, ROBINSON, HAMMERSHAIMB, MAAG and others. WEISER, *op. cit.*, p. 41 adds vs. 7. NEHER, *Amos*, (Paris, 1950), p. 126 puts vss. 1-6 together. EDGEHILL, *The Book of Amos*, *W.C.* (1914), p. 98 constructs an account using

As to literary style, the accounts display excellence, vigor and compact expression as well as highly polished form. This latter binds the first four accounts together and shows how they are related to each other. Deeper analysis also reveals the connection with the. fifth.

The introductory, "Thus the Lord Jahweh showed me," [1] is identical in the first four visions. [2] This and the following "and behold" more than anything else show the fixed form in which the visions are repeated. The fifth vision has the shorter, "I saw," as its only introduction. [3]

The second element in the visions begins "and behold" and goes on to describe the content of the vision. This is naturally the most complex and varied part of the accounts. [4] This section may be further analysed into two or three parts: the object or scene which is seen (locusts, fire, a plumb line, a basket of summer fruit, crumbling pillars); progression or action (I and II), [5] dialogue to emphasize the object (III and IV), [6] or a command to action (V); [7] an explanation of the vision's meaning (only in the last three). [8]

The third element indicates the prophet's role [9] in the event. In the first two visions he appears as intercessor for his people. [10] The other visions leave no room for this activity since God says, "I shall

---

ix 1, iii 14 and vii 9. Using a common theme as a basis for asserting literary unity is a method which can only be branded as arbitrary.

[1] Cf. L. H. BROCKINGTON, "'The Lord Showed Me' The Correlation of Natural and Spiritual in Prophetic Experience," *S.H.R.*, p. 30 ff.; G. HÖLSCHER, *Die Propheten* (Leipzig, 1914), p. 198; RUDOLPH, *op. cit.*, p. 21; F. HÄUSERMANN, *Wortempfang und Symbol in den alttestamentlichen Propheten* (*B.Z.A.W.* LVIII, Giessen, 1923), pp. 34, 69, 80; J. HÄNEL, *Das Erkennen Gottes bei den Schrift-Propheten* (*B.Z.A.W.* n.f. IV, Stuttgart, 1923), pp. 98, 105, 126; R. S. CRIPPS, *Critical and Exegetical Commentary on the Book of Amos* (2nd. ed., London, 1955), pp. 91 ff., 100 ff., 218 ff.

[2] Amos vii 1; vii 4; viii 1. The 3rd (vii 7) has a shortened form: "He showed me." Cf. Jer. xxiv 1 ff.

[3] Amos ix 1.

[4] Cf. H. S. MACKENZIE, "The plumb-line: Amos vii 8," *Ex. T.* LX (1949), p. 159.

[5] Amos vii 2 and vii 4b.

[6] Amos vii 8a and viii 2a.

[7] Amos ix 1 and 4a.

[8] Amos vii 8b, viii 2b and ix 4b.

[9] Note that he is not simply a passive visionary, but an active participant in the vision as well as being called through the vision to fulfill a task.

[10] See above p. 11, n. 152b. Here he already acts as a prophet. These cannot then be viewed as predating Amos' call as WEISER thinks. Cf. HERNTRICH, *Amos, der Prophet Gottes* (1941), p. 70.

not pass over them again." [1] It should be quite clear that this section does not designate the entire role which the prophet must fill, [2] but only the one directly related to God.

(4)   The fourth element of the visions brings each to a close with an indication of God's decision concerning what happens next. The first two visions show the effective intercession of the prophet and the promise of grace on the part of God. [3] The following pair show God's firm decision to bring judgement which he will not change. [4] And this latter decision is strongly supported by the fifth vision. [5]

A superfical examination of identical phrases reveals two pairs of visions [6] and a somewhat different final account. [7] Deeper analysis shows a common formula behind all five: [8] introduction—identical in four, similar in the fifth; body of vision: describes what is seen and heard, including indication of the meaning; and finally indications of the prophet's role and God's attitude which remains.

It is to be noted that the second vision is joined to the first not only by similarity of form but by the "also" in verse 4 as well. The third vision also is joined to the first two since it obviously forms the climax toward which they point. Its "I shall not pass over them again" quite definitely is intended as an antithesis to the two accounts of forgiveness which precede it. The first three visions, then, form a unit (as their position in the book would imply) and were intended to be spoken at the same time. [9]

Although the fourth vision is like the others in its form and points back to them, its message adds nothing really new and should be understood as a confirmation of the judgement spoken in the third vision. [10] The first three visions can be understood very well as

---

[1] Amos vii 8b, vii 2b and ix 4b.

[2] There is nothing said, for instance, about his message to the people. But certainly there must be a relation understood to exist between the vision and the message of the prophet.

[3] Amos vii 3 and vii 6.

[4] Amos vii 8c and viii 2b.

[5] Amos ix 4b.

[6] Amos viii 1-3 with vss. 4-6; vii 7-9 with viii 1-3; Cf. W. RIEDEL, *Alttestamentliche Untersuchungen* (Leipzig, 1902), p. 27 f.

[7] Amos ix 1 ff.

[8] See attached chart.

[9] In this way they might very well be thought of as an introduction to his preaching at Bethel.

[10] GORDIS, *op. cit.*, pp. 250-51, note 31 presents arguments for separating the fourth from the previous three visions.

forming a unit to themselves. However, one can hardly think of the fourth vision as being spoken without the first three going before. [1]

Can it be then that those who view the biographical account of vii 10-17 as a literary intrusion [2] are both right and wrong? that the visions were spoken both in a version of three and then later in a version of four? [3] If so, the placing of the biographical section in its present location may have more meaning that has generally been granted it. [4] However this may be, the bonds which bind these four visions are strong enough for us to conclude that the version which finds expression in our book is the later one consisting of all four accounts. [5]

The fifth vision is less closely connected than the fourth, [6] but its relation may be exactly that of the fourth. [7] A new message or element is not to be found there, yet there is a certain progression, [8] and one can hardly conceive its presentation without the previous four leading up to it.

This suggests that Visions I to III, which were once presented as a unit, were later repeated with the addition of Vision IV. These four were at still a third occasion recited as a prelude to the fifth. But we have noted above that a series of prophetic "words" [9] separates the final two visions, while a biographic account of the prophet's appearance in Bethel has intruded itself along with a fragmentary "word" [10] after the third. What is their relation to the "Visions"?

---

[1] There is a finality about this fourth vision which rings true only when the intercession and struggle of the others is presupposed.

[2] HEMPEL, *op. cit.*, p. 129, for example, speaks about the visions being broken apart by interruptions.

[3] Indicating the "Sitz im Leben" of the first three at Bethel, but designating the fourth as belonging to a later period, a different place. But when this fourth one was spoken at a southern sanctuary, perhaps a year later, the first three were repeated as an introduction to it.

[4] Being the key to this distinction.

[5] In this I am siding with WEISER against Gordis. Cf. RUDOLPH, *op. cit.*, p. 20. WEISER's contention (p. 26), that the last line of visions III and IV cannot be Amos' goal in telling the visions because these last two are parallel, overlooks this possibility of their original proclamation first in a group of three and only later as four.

[6] Its different form and pace mark this looseness.

[7] I.e. It is *not* necessary to them, but they *are* necessary as introductions to its presentation.

[8] But this is a far cry from the "einheitliche Zielrichtung" towards the earthquake which WEISER (p. 250) assumes.

[9] Amos viii 4-14.

[10] Amos vii 10-17.

B. RELATION OF VISION AND BIOGRAPHY [1]

The visions reflect the prophet's experience with God. But it is obvious that he must also deal with men and society in presenting that which God had revealed to him in his vision. It is then not unthinkable [2] that the story of the reception which a prophet received should find a place beside the account of his experience of God.

However, the similar form of the first four visions has led most interpreters to regard them as a unit [3] and view this biographical account as a bit of foreign matter which does not belong here. [4] Various more suitable positions have been suggested, [5] but there has been no general acceptance of any one of them.

If, as has been suggested above, there is no necessity to think of the four visions as having *originally* formed a unit, the question inevitably rises whether this biographical passage cannot be justifiably left and interpreted where it is, and whether its presence at just this place does not have significance for our understanding of Amos. [6]

It has often been suggested that the basis for its placement here is the similarity between Amaziah's report and the "word" fragment in vs. 9. [7] Since the presence of vs. 9 at this point is also left unexplained by this theory, [8] it cannot be regarded as satisfactory. Vs. 9 will be dealt with below. [9]

Two questions were left unanswered in the discussion above: When were the visions seen and reported? and where? If vii 10-17 has any significance for our study of the visions, it must be in suggesting an answer to these questions. [10]

---

[1] Here Amos vii 1-9; viii 1-3 and vii 10-17. But the question of the relation of the two types of prophetic literature is to be kept in mind throughout.

[2] As most comments seem to imply.

[3] BUDDE, *op. cit.*, p. 63; id., *Wellhausen Festschrift* (1914), p. 65 ff.

[4] One may gladly agree with WEISER (p. 264) that vii 10-17 is different from the vision accounts and secondary to them. Its very form reveals that much.

[5] H. GRESSMANN, *Die älteste Geschichtsschreibung und Prophetie Israels*, S.A.T. II (1921), p. 330 relates it to the biographical notice in i 1-2 and prints it after this passage. EDGEHILL, *op. cit.*, p. 98 would place it after the last vision. SELLIN-ROST, *Einleitung in das Alte Testament* (Heidelberg, 1950), p. 128 suggests the end of ch. vi. CRIPPS, *op. cit.*, p. 311 looks favorably on a position after ch. iii.

[6] GORDIS' arguments and results are applicable here, although the conclusions he draws concerning the formation of the book must be rejected.

[7] Cf. BENTZEN, *Introduction to the Old Testament* II (Copenhagen, 1949), p. 140 and many others.

[8] Separated as it is from the actual vision, vss. 7-8.

[9] P. 47.

[10] If its presence is to be explained as anything more than literary accident.

Far deeper and more important than the similarity between vss. 9 and 10 is the obvious indication of an intended relation of biography and vision. Their juxtaposition indicates that vision set the stage for Amos' message at Bethel which earned him his expulsion. [1] It may suggest that these visions were recited there [2] and that the fragment of his message [3] was spoken there on the occasion related here.

The apparent intention of the account is to tell of the end of Amos' ministry at Bethel [4] and presumably in the Northern Kingdom [5] because he was put out of the country on orders of Amaziah.

Here then we have the setting for the third vision at a great festival [6] in Bethel just before the *end* [7] of Amos' ministry there. This vision marked the tone and message on which he closed his ministry there, not that on which he began it. [8] The beginning of his ministry was on the basis of his call to be a prophet to Israel with no reference to the nature of his message. [9] But by the time he preached in Bethel that last time, he had been given to see judgement without mercy as the sign of Israel's future. [10]

The order and obvious progression of the visions suggest that the first two visions reflect experiences and periods which preceded the third. [11] They must have characterized earlier periods of his ministry just as this final decisive period is reflected in the third vision.

An acceptance of the present position of the biographical section implies that the following visions and messages came after that

---

[1] Amos vii 12.

[2] Cf. above, p. 31, note 3.

[3] Vs. 9.

[4] Cf. WEISER, *op. cit.*, p. 261. Others have suggested that the account only serves to introduce the prophet's speech in vs. 17. Still others suggest that it is the remaining fragment of what was once a complete biography of the prophet.

[5] There is no evidence for a return or continued activity there. I Kings xiii may hardly be presented as evidence for such even if a connection with Amos could be established.

[6] The importance of Bethel as a royal sanctuary would be immeasurably heightened if the occasion were a royal festival.

[7] Cf. Amos vii 8, 13 and viii 2.

[8] E. SELLIN, *Das Zwölfprophetenbuch* (3rd. ed., Leipzig, 1929), p. 253 views the visions as a unit saying that they caused the expulsion from Bethel. Therefore, vii 10-17 must originally have stood at the end of the visions. Cf. also GORDIS, *op. cit.*, p. 240.

[9] See above, p. 22, note 9.

[10] Amos: vii 8: "I will never pass by them again."

[11] The increasing harshness of judgement with the move from receptiveness to intercession to unreceptiveness suggests this.

fateful day at Bethel. [1] If the festival at which Amos appeared in Bethel was that of the New Year, [2] the implication would be that a repetition [3] of the visions with the addition of the fourth would fit in a New Year's setting, perhaps a year later at some Judaean sanctuary. [4] The final vision could very well have been spoken and experienced (for there experience and recital seem to have been much closer together) [5] on the second anniversary of his ejection from Bethel. [6] Thus, each succeeding year Amos recited the earlier visions as reports of the message which had been given to him and added the latest one as a verification and confirmation. [7]

If there is truth in this interpretation, may not the "two years before the earthquake" of 1 : 1 date the great appearance at Bethel as exactly two years before the earthquake fulfillment [8] recounted in the fifth vision? [9] That might give us a date of 752 B.C. for the third

---

[1] GORDIS' conclusion (*op. cit.*, p. 250) that Amos' expulsion led him to the conviction that there was not the slightest ground for hope that Israel could be saved overlooks the severity and finality implied in the judgement spoken in the third vision. However, there can be no doubt that his expulsion confirmed the decision he had heard in the preceding vision.

[2] As MORGENSTERN contends: "Amos Studies", *H.U.C.A.* XII-XIII (1937-38), p. 46.

[3] Amos' activity in connection with a harvest festival would make repetition at later festivals natural if not necessary.

[4] McCULLOUGH, "Some Suggestions about Amos," *J.B.L.* LXXII (1953), p. 250 intimates that Amos vii 12 "suggests the possibility of a ministry in the South." His reappearance at a southern sanctuary repeating the vision accounts with the addition of this last would give the substance of such a ministry. GORDIS maintains the impossible position that chs. viii-ix were spoken in the north (*op. cit.*, p. 247). Surely KÖHLER, *Amos, der älteste Schriftprophet* (Zürich, 1920), p. 43, is more nearly right in saying that the story implies that he had to leave the northern kingdom for good. T. K. CHEYNE, *E.B.* I (London, 1899), col. 154 even suggests that Amos visited Jerusalem after his expulsion from Bethel. Cf. also BUTTENWIESER, *The Prophets of Israel* (Chicago, 1914), pp. 232-36; N. H. SNAITH, *Amos, Part I: Study Notes on Bible Books* (London, 1945), pp. 34-36. CRIPPS, *op. cit.*, pp. 12-14.

For the fantastic suppositions of R. E. WOLFE, *Meet Amos and Hosea* (N.Y., 1945), pp. 60-61, that Amos was martyred at Bethel there is not a shred of evidence.

[5] The very juxtaposition of the two as well as the subject matter indicated that.

[6] Or at a greater interval, as I suggested in *Ex. T.* LXVI (1955), p. 111 for the following speeches. But see below.

[7] Or added speeches of application or amplification.

[8] MORGENSTERN, "Amos Studies I," *H.U.C.A.* XI (1936), p. 140 equates this with the event in II Chronicles xxvi 16-21 which is traditionally said to have been accompanied by a great earthquake.

[9] Amos ix 1 appears to portray a judgement actually taking place.

vision and the Bethel ministry with 750 B.C. for the final vision. [1]

Thus the placement of vii 10-17 at this point answers important questions concerning the "when" and the "where" of the visions and indicates a Judaean ministry [2] for Amos at the close of that in Israel.

C. RELATION OF VISION AND "WORD"

Weiser's great contribution lay in studying the visions as reflections of true experiences [3] as well as rhetorical masterpieces. [4] Each vision must then be treated separately to delineate both the experience which it depicts and the message which resulted from it.

In regard to the experience reflected, it should be noted that Amos appears [5] in these visions as a prophet. [6] This is especially true of the very first two where the prophet intercedes [7] for Israel. Their purpose is then not to explain how Amos became a prophet, [8] but to explain

---

[1] This is dependent upon the dating of Jotham's regency. MORGENSTERN, as we have seen above, equates that date with the earthquake in Amos i 1 and ix 1. He accepts 750-49 B.C. as the consensus of scholarly opinion. BEGRICH, *Chronologie der Könige von Israel und Judah* (1929), p. 155 presents alternative possibilities: either 758-757 or 747-746. ALBRIGHT, *B.A.S.O.R.* (Dec. 1945) dates it at 750, and he is followed by the 2nd edition of the *Westminster Atlas*, ed. by WRIGHT and FILSON (Philadelphia, 1956). MONTGOMERY-GEHMAN, *Kings, I.C.C.* (Edinburgh, 1951) lists it as 751. THIELE, *The Mysterious numbers of the Hebrew Kings* (Chicago, 1951) has Jotham's regency beginning in 750, but throws all the reckoning in regard to Amos out of joint by insisting that Joroboam II died in 753. A. CARLIER, *La Chronologie des Rois de Juda et d'Israël* (Paris, 1953), pp. 40-41 suggests alternate possibilities in 750 and 748. His dating of Amos (beginning 754) fits this scheme also. N. SNAITH, *Mercy and Sacrifice* (London, 1953), p. 12 has the latest date of all: 744. We follow ALBRIGHT, MONTGOMERY, and THIELE in placing the beginning of Jotham's regency in 750, thus making the date of Amos' appearance at Bethel 752 B.C.

[2] By the clear implication that his ministry in Bethel and the Northern Kingdom closed after this experience and the indications that the visions in Chs. viii and ix must come after and build upon those in Ch. vii.

[3] WEISER, *op. cit.*, p. 2.

[4] *Ibid.* Therefore the two matters of experience and composition must be dealt with separately. Cf. RUDOLPH, *op. cit.*, p. 25. But with WEISER we should understand the visions as being prepared for oral rendition rather than simply as literary productions as G. HÖLSCHER, *Geschichte der israelitischen und jüdischen Religion* (Giessen, 1922), p. 104, note 3, and PROCKSCH, *Die Kleinen prophetischen Schriften vor dem Exil* (1910), p. 87 indicate.

[5] By his observation and part in the dialogue.

[6] One who shares the counsel of God (Amos iii 7).

[7] Amos vii 2 and vii 5.

[8] As WEISER, *op. cit.*, p. 68-69 seems to indicate.

and authenticate his message. [1] They should then be interpreted in closest relation to the messages. *What is the relation then between Vision* [2] *(Experience) and Message in Amos?* For an answer let us examine chapter 8 in which both "Vision" and "Messages" appear.

The vision which introduces the chapter is short, compact, and simple in form. The object of the vision is simply a kĕlūb qảyĭtz, "a basket of summer fruit." [3] The object is simple enough [4] and there is no further description of it. But this simplicity should not blind us to the wealth of meaning wrapped up in this short designation.

It tells us that the time of year was the fall, the end of the hot dry summer period. This period was "the end" of the year for Near Easterners in the same sense that winter ends our year. [5] The ground was parched and burnt bare. The fruit of trees hardy enough to survive the heat had ripened and been gathered, and now the bare trees stood out against the stark brown of the landscape. All nature and all people yearned for the coming rains which the fall equinox should bring with refreshing cool, reviving moisture, and joyful entry into another year. [6] Ugaritic myths for this season tell of the reign of the king of summer (q ẓ) [7] who was responsible for summer's devastation, and who would be unseated by the god of the sea (yằm) [8]

---

[1] Not in the sense of BAUMANN's "vindication," but to undergird the certainty of it and the call to repentence that grows from it (Cf. WÜRTHWEIN, *op. cit.*, pp. 34-35).

[2] In the double sense of experience and the account of it.

[3] Jer. xxiv is often cited as a parallel, but the words are completely different as is the meaning. Cf. D. BALY, *The Geography of the Bible* (New York, 1957), p. 103.

[4] Surely something to be commonly met with in Israel and Judah during the fall harvest.

[5] The New Year was reckoned from the period when the autumnal rains were expected.

[6] M. NOTH, *Die Welt des Alten Testaments* (2nd. ed. 1953), pp. 24-25.

[7] *U.H.* LXXVI, 17, 25; *U.L.*, pp. 63-65; *C.M.*, pp. 124-127. The implication that the wedding of the moon god will bring the fertile rains with the god of summer being called upon to approve or make possible the wedding is clear even if the form in which it is found here is that of a wedding poem. The character of the king of summer is disputed. The proper name of the king is ḥarḥab. If this may be understood to be kin to the Hebrew hrb (be dry, waste, or desolate), then the question is decided. He represents the death of vegetation characteristic of the long dry summer. Cf. T. H. GASTER, *Thespis* (N.Y., 1950), p. 124; A. S. KAPELRUD, *Baal in the Ras Shamra Texts* (Copenhagen, 1952), p. 81.

Unfortunately this king of summer is not mentioned in other texts. In the Baal cycle II col. viii and I *Môt*, god of the underworld fills this role.

[8] God of seas and streams. Baal cycle III A, B, C.

in the autumnal storms. [1] And finally they relate the resurrection of life and power of Ba'al [2] in the coming of the fall rains. These myths fitted into the dramatic ritual of the fall New Year's festival when the low spirits of a people tired of the burning summer found expression in their ritual mourning [3] for that which had died (nature represented in Ba'al). These Canaanite festivals like those of the Babylonians were considered to be the occasion at which the gods settled everyone's fate for the new year. [4] Every effort was made to assure a favorable oracle for the coming year. [5] For the people as a whole this meant oracles of peace and victory, [6] of rain and plenty, [7] of light and joy. [8] When these rituals and oracles produced the proper results through sympathetic magic and careful calculation, the joy of the people knew no bounds of ecstasy and song.

---

[1] GASTER, op. cit., p. 118 is supported by HOOKE, JOHS. PEDERSEN, ENGNELL, MOWINCKEL in the view that these are cult texts representing an annual celebration of the return of rain. GORDON, U.L., pp. 3-5, DRIVER, C.M., p. 20, and others have protested that the Baal cycle is not to be understood as reflecting an annual process. Gordon seems to incline toward a seven year cycle. Their protests correctly point to a lack of textual evidence for such an interpretation. Yet neither of them provides an appropriate "Sitz im Leben" which is not seasonal. (Cf. KAPELRUD's discussion, op. cit., pp. 13-27, 128). They all agree however with Gaster's interpretation in terms of the relative merits of different kinds of irrigation.

The climax of both the Nikkal and Baal cycles concerns the coming of rain following the reign of summer. The movement of events in the two is quite different, however. How are they related to each other? KAPELRUD's conclusions that they are "cult texts" and are "related to fertility" seem to be born out. But they are different in that the Nikkal texts are concerned throughout with moon dieties while the Baal cycle shows no such orientation. In the Nikkal text the moon goddess is preferred to the daughter of Baal (NK I 25-II 3). Cf. KAPELRUD, op. cit., p. 81. Can it be that this reflects a rivalry between competing cults? On the one hand the claims of the moon cults that fertility is ensured in the calm return of the season by the marriage of lunar deities. On the other hand the claims of the Baal cult that through his victory and resurrection the rains return. If this is true, the contention that ḫarḫab and môt fill the same role gains credence.

[2] Baal cycle IV.

[3] U.H. text 67; A.N.E.T. IAB p. 138 ff.; C.M. p. 109. Comparisons to other weeping cults can be conveniently made by referring to KAPELRUD, op. cit., pp. 27-47.

[4] GASTER, op. cit., p. 349; KAPELRUD, op. cit., p. 139.

[5] T. H. GASTER, "The Religion of the Canaanites," Forgotten Religions (ed. V. Ferm, N.Y., 1950), p. 117 ff.; S. MOWINCKEL,, Religion und Kultus (Göttingen, 1953), p. 58.

[6] Celebration of Baal as victor over the sea C.M. B III iii; as victor over môt B V iii-iv.

[7] C.M. B IV i 5, 13, 14; III iii 6-13.

[8] C.M. NK II 10.

Exactly what Israelitic festivals were like during the kingdom we do not know. [1] But there are many signs that they had absorbed Canaanite practices [2] so that Jahwistic ritual and custom had been distorted almost beyond recognition. This would have been especially true at Bethel, [3] but it is likely that the main features could have been found at any one of the Israelitic sanctuaries of this period.

If Amos' "basket of summer fruit" was a real object [4] (not simply a vision), it indicated that the harvest was in progress or past. Hence, the New Year Festival was near. [5] Perhaps Amos was already on his pilgrimage toward the sanctuary with most of Judah. [6] In this word *qăyĭts* "summer" there also could be heard a little of the impatience with heat and drought in the hope for a change of season.

But it was Jahweh's explanation which provided a key to Amos' vision. [7] The summer fruit was not simply a sign of the end of summer, the end of a condition distasteful to the people. Quite the opposite!

> "When Jahweh said, "What do you see Amos?"
> I said, "A basket of summer fruit." (*qăyĭts*)
> Then Jahweh said to me,
> "The end (*qēts*) has come to my people Israel!
> I shall never pass by them again!" (viii 2)

It was the *end*, not of a disagreeable season, but of God's people, Israel, which was intended. [8] Judgement had been determined.

---

[1] PEDERSEN, *Israel III-IV*, p. 737 ff.; R. HENTSCHKE, *Die Stellung der vorexilischen Schriftpropheten zum Kultus* (*B.Z.A.W.* 75, Berlin, 1957).

[2] S. MOWINCKEL, *Religion und Kultus*, p. 70 f.

[3] Jeroboam's golden bull is ample sign of it.

[4] E. A. EDGEHILL, *op. cit.*, p. 80.

[5] Despite the arguments of L. I. PAP, *Das Israelitische Neujahrsfest* (Kampen, 1933); N. SNAITH, *The Jewish New Year Festival* (London, 1947), W. S. MC CULLOUGH, "Israel's Kings Sacral *and otherwise*," *Ex. T.* LXVIII (Feb. 1957), pp. 144-48 and many elements of the theses of S. MOWINCKEL, *Psalmenstudien II* (Kristiana, 1922) and VOLZ, *Das Neujahrsfest Jahwes* (Tübingen, 1912) find convinced adherents. Cf. H. J. KRAUS, *Gottesdienst in Israel* (München, 1954); A. R. JOHNSON, *Sacral Kingship in Ancient Israel* (Cardiff, 1955); G. WIDENGREN, *Sakrales Königtum im Alten Testament und im Judentum* (Stuttgart, 1955).

[6] Amos testifies to the pilgrimage customs of his time iv 4-5; v 5.

[7] This important element characterizes only the third and fourth visions.

[8] HENTSCHKE's observation (*op. cit.*, p. 53) that Amos' conviction of God's free sovereignty could not be reconciled to the bonds of current cult practice is accurate. But it is not evident that he envisioned any real existence of Israel in which personal, socioethical relations should take the place of the ritual now under judgement. He does attack the whole ritual (cf. p. 73) but he announces judgement on *Israel*, not simply on the *cultus*. The basis for the *cultus* as indeed for Israel's very existence was the covenant which was now under judgement.

There would be no renewal. [1] There would be no forgiveness. [2] Judgement had fallen, and whatever ritual or prophecy might indicate the opposite was empty and untrue. [3] God had spoken.

We have already indicated above that this was the end of the clearly-marked form of the vision. Vs. 3 is not a continuation or an addition to the vision in either form or content. [4] Yet it cannot be an independent "message" for it is clearly dependent on something which must have gone before it. It reads: "And the songs (of joy) of the temple shall become howlings (of grief) in that day,' the Lord Jahweh's own expression." (viii)

"In that day" is a reference to the great Day of Jahweh on which he would judge and save. [5] It is generally clear in the prophets that this day is future and of a unique character. But there are a number of indications that popular usage related it to the New Year's portents of what the following year would bring. Properly celebrated,[6] in Israel the day (New Year's day) [7] was one in which under Jahweh's judgement, [8] the people confessed their sins, [9] offered sacrifices, [10] and renewed the covenant with Jahweh [11] in full consciousness of his election and his righteous demands upon them. [12] If this is so, thoughts

---

[1] Cf. Kraus, *Gottesdienst in Israel*, p. 93. Renewal of the relation to God in the heart of the festival.

[2] Cf. Amos vii 8 and viii 2 "I shall never pass by them again!"

[3] Opposition of this sort is not found here. But other prophets encountered it. Cf. Jer. xxviii and 1 Kings xxii 17-28.

[4] Weiser, *op. cit.*, p. 258.

[5] See the discussion in chapter IV.

[6] This assumes the view that cult could be positively viewed, but that the effects of its current practice were to be condemned.

[7] Hentschke, *op. cit.*, p. 25-26 properly questions Schmidt's interpretation (*Die Thronfahrt Jahwes*, p. 46) of Amos v 26-27. But he certainly leaps beyond the evidence when he asserts that the prophets never refer to dramatic cult forms.

[8] Cf. A. Weiser, *Die Psalmen* (*A.T.D.*, Göttingen, 1950), p. 16.

[9] Cf. H. J. Kraus, *op. cit.*, p. 95 f.

[10] It may be assumed that sacrifice played an important part in all ritual, as the Old Testament testifies.

[11] L. Rost, "Sinaibund und Davidsbund," *T.L.Z.* (1947), p. 130 contends that this applies both to Israel and to Judah.

G. Widengren, "King and Covenant," *J.S.S.* II (1957), pp. 1-32.

[12] Johnson, *op. cit.*, p. 92 looking at the matter from a different viewpoint lists these as the effects of the dramatic festival: a) an assurance of final victory over 'Death' . . . b) a summons to a renewal of faith in Yahweh . . . c) a challenge to a renewed endeavor to be faithful to him. R. Bach, "Gottesrecht und weltliches Recht in der Verkündigung des Propheten Amos," *Festschrift für Günther Dehn*, pp. 23-34 makes clear that these righteous demands were those of the "apodictic" law.

of "that day" were in everyone's mind. Concern for Jahweh's favorable reaction to their worship was expressed by religious people at least, and a prophet's message would be expected for that day. [1]

Amos' message was clearly one of "darkness and not light" for that day. [2] Instead of the usual order in which the grief and mourning which characterized the earlier portions (or days) of the festival [3] turned into joy and praise through the signs that God had accepted his people again, that he would bless them, and that the rains would again turn "death into life" in their fields, the songs of joy would now be turned into grief with its accompanying ceremonies. This would surely have been the order of events if instead of a "renewal" of the covenant with its provisions of ritual, intercession, and grace, at the ceremony's climax, God simply declared an "end" to this relation of election with "his people, Israel." [4]

This fragmentary message certainly *fits the mood* of the vision even if the form of the vision forbids viewing it as a *part* of it. [5] It should be noted that the fragmentary message is impersonally stated, while the vision is in the first person and the following passage in the second person plural. [6]

Vss. 4-6 form another of those accusations against the rich for ruthless and unjust actions. [7] Amos spoke directly to them in his own words (not indicating that they are from Jahweh) and with his accustomed vigor. In vs. 5 he evidently addressed people in or near the sanctuary who were most uncomfortable at having to close their businesses for even one day of the festival. [8] They were so engrossed in their schemes for cheating and stealing that they had no thought for ceremonies and sermons. [9]

---

[1] He must fill the role of the "Bundesmittler." Cf. KRAUS, *op. cit.*, p. 59.

[2] Amos v 18.

[3] There is no agreement about the order of events. MOWINCKEL speaks of Jahweh's enthronement as the climax and end of the festival. JOHNSON characterizes the Jerusalem festival as beginning on that note, then showing periods of struggle and distress and returning to a note of victory. This latter order seems to do justice to the Psalm material and is more acceptable here as well.

[4] CRAMER, *Amos* (Stuttgart, 1930), p. 94.

[5] See the discussion of form above.

[6] Thus they cannot have been originally conceived as spoken together. Although the different parts are all related to the same event and prophecy, their present arrangement is artificial and must be explained by a pattern which molded them together giving them both form and meaning.

[7] WEISER, *op. cit.*, pp. 27 and 258.

[8] Amos viii.

[9] Amos viii 4-6.

Vss. 7-8 draw a direct connection between their way of life and this judgement. [1] Jahweh has sworn [2] never to forget (nor forgive) their deeds. This verse is not simply a continuation of vss. 4-6. It does not speak in the second person, but in the third. Yet it is clear that vs. 7 is spoken with these wrong-doers in mind. [3]

Vs. 8 is closely connected to vs. 7. [4] Vs. 7 repeats of a word directly from Jahweh. [5] Vs. 8 is a word from the prophet which draws a conclusion from this Jahweh "word." [6]

The first part is a question which must be translated, "Is it because of this that the land does not tremble (quiver)?" [7] The word *rāgāz* (tremble) is usually interpreted as an earthquake. [8] But in this setting that is impossible. The passage both in time of year and in literary context is one dealing with drought and rain, i.e. fertility. A parallel in ix 5 is a reaction to Jahweh's "touching the earth." [9] The "tremble" seems to be the earth's reaction to Jahweh's blessing. [10] The question asks if the earth's failure to respond, quivering with new life, to the expected change of season is not traceable to God's judgement upon the people's sins just mentioned. [11]

The second line pictures a scene of mass mourning. If the interpretation in terms of rain and fertility is correct, this must mean ritual mourning. [12] The whole should be understood in antithesis to the previous line: "Although every inhabitant mourn in (with) her." Such mourning rites were common in Near Eastern cultures in

---

[1] This stress on the relevance of ethical dealing to worship is, of course, one of Amos' outstanding characteristics.

[2] The formula is used of Jahweh's oath to Abraham (Gen. xxii 16 and many others) and of his oath to David II Sam. iii 9; Ps. lxxxix 3. But it is also used frequently in the prophets concerning His purposes and His decisions.

[3] Cf. "their deeds."

[4] Cf. also ix 5 and the discussion of it on ch. III, p. 51, n. 49.

[5] Introduced by the formula, "Jahweh has sworn."

[6] Although the close parallel to the hymn fragment in ix 5 shows that the words are familiar ones.

[7] The usual translation, "Shall not the land tremble on this account?" (R.S.V.) is grammatically impossible. The question is on the phrase "because of this" rather than on the negative particle which only comes with the verb at the end of the sentence.

[8] WEISER, *op. cit.*, pp. 30 and 258; RIEDEL, *op. cit.*, pp. 33-34.

[9] See chapter III p. 50. There the word is "quiver".

[10] Not the result of His judgement.

[11] Vs. 7 and vss. 4-6.

[12] Cf. David's mourning with the hope of saving his son, II Sam. xii 15; PEDERSEN, *Israel III-IV*, p. 455-461.

relation to the drought of summer. [1] They assumed the form of worship and prayer that the life of nature might return. [2] This was the mourning which should turn to gladness through the course of the festival, but which the prophet predicted would be turned back to real and bitter grief.

The following line with its comparison to the Nile [3] can hardly be a reference to violence. [4] The Nile is a classic figure for fertility. [5] The verbs describe a rise, spread, and irrigation like that of the Nile. But what is it that does these? *Kŭllāh* is usually translated "all of it." [6] But that makes no sense in the context of our interpretation. [7] This context would demand something like "water" for the subject. [8] For Palestine that must be artificial irrigation which is exactly what the word *shaqah* would indicate. [9] Various words built on the root *kăl* have the idea of "containing." [10] *Kăllāh*, bride, has the sense of one reserved, protected. [11] *Kūl* might be derived from *kālāh* as *kĕlīj*, "vessel," and have the meaning "contents, or saved up parts." This would make excellent sense in denoting water preserved in cisterns or containers such as were standard equipment in Canaanite and Israelite sanctuaries. [12]

The description must have been of a cult practice which accompanied or followed the mourning. In imitation of the practice of irrigation, water was drawn up and the altar area was drenched with a libation of water. [13] The practice may be reflected in the story of

---

[1] Assuming the form of "weeping for Tammuz" Ez. viii 14 or Adonis.

[2] Cf. A. S. KAPELRUD, *op. cit.*, pp. 121-122.

[3] Following the reading of the versions and the parallel in ix 5.

[4] The Nile's flood is no tragedy to Egypt, but blessing. The rise is slow and regular with none of the catastrophic connotations of floods in other countries.

[5] Cf. A.N.E.T., p. 370.—"But God (Re) has made a Nile in Heaven for other peoples."

[6] The noun *Kôl* with a 3rd. person feminine pronominal suffix.

[7] "The earth" does not "rise like the Nile" instead of the hoped-for "trembling."

[8] As a parallel to the "Nile."

[9] GASTER, *op. cit.*, p. 123, n. 13. Ugaritic myths speak of an interrex of Ashtar, god of artificial irrigation. Cf. p. 126 f and 196 f.; G. R. DRIVER, *Canaanite Myths and Legends*, pp. 20-21. In Ps. lxv 10, *Shāqāh* is correctly written and should be translated as "irrigate it" in accordance with its meaning in the cognate languages.

[10] כְּלִי, כְּלָל, כְּלָא etc.

[11] Cf. KÖHLER, *Lexicon in Veteris Testamenti Libros*, p. 438.

[12] PEDERSEN, *op. cit.*, pp. 201, 228.

[13] PEDERSEN, *op. cit.*, p. 197; L. FEUCHTWANG, "Das Wasseropfer und die damit verbundenen Zeremonien," *M.G.W.J.* LIV (1910), pp. 535-552, 713-729.

Elijah on Mount Carmel. [1] He had the altar and its contents soaked with water and a trench. [2] around the altar filled to the brim. The mourning rites are there pictured graphically in the orgies of the Ba'al priests. [3]

The verse should then read:

"Is it on account of this that the land does not respond? Although every inhabitant has mourned in (with) her. And her treasured contents (cistern water) have flowed up like the Nile, been spread about, and have irrigated like the Nile of Egypt?" (viii 8)

Vss. 9 and 10 are introduced with the phrase: "And it shall happen in that day." As noted above this would be the high point of a prophet's message at that time of year. It was a prediction of God's response to their prayer and ritual. But, as also noted before, the prophet's predictions often dealt with issues far deeper and more final. His prediction was dark:

"And it shall happen in that day," expression of the Lord Jahweh "that I shall bring in the sun at noon and darken the earth in the daytime.
I shall turn feasts into mourning and all your songs to lamentations.
I shall put sacking undergarments on evergone and cause heads to be shaved bald.
I shall constitute it like a mourning for an only child [4] and the end of it like a bitter day." (viii 9-10)

If this has a familiar ring, note that we have just read a short summary of it in vs. 3. Here is the full message of that Day "which is darkness and not light." A Day in which the bright promise of the morning would fade into panic and despair because twilight and

---

[1] N. SNAITH, *I.B.* III, p. 158; J. MORGENSTERN, "Amos Studies III," *H.U.C.A.* XV (1940), pp. 182-185; *Id.*, "Two Ancient Agricultural Festivals," *J.Q.R.* VIII (1917), pp. 31-54; Id., "Three Calendars of Ancient Israel," *H.U.C,A.* I (1924), pp. 13-78; Id., "Supplementary Studies in the Calendars of Ancient Israel," *H.U.C.A.* X (1935), pp. 1-148; PATAI, "Control of Rain in Ancient Palestine," *H.U.C.A.* XIV (1939), pp. 254-260; J. PEDERSEN, *Israel III-IV* (Copenhagen, 1940), pp. 517, 520; *Id.* pp. 342-43; and II Sam. xxiii 16.

[2] I Kings xviii 32 ff.

[3] GASTER, *Forgotten Religious*, p. 131.

[4] MOVERS, *Die Phönizier I*, p. 248 f. and others have understood the *yāhīd* (only child) to refer to mourning for Adonis as an example of a great day of mourning. But BAUDISSIN, *Adonis und Esmun* (Leipzig, 1911), p. 89 doubts this because Adonis is never referred to as "the only one." A possible identification may be found in Philo Byblius who in his commentary on Isaac's offering calls Isaac a *yahid*. Cf. also Jer. vi 26 and Zech. xii 10. The lack of an article seems to rule out a reference to Adonis. Cf. however, DRIVER, *Canaanite Myths*, p. 17 where he comments on *Ydd bn 'el* as an appelation for *Môt*.

darkness would descend by noon. The verses describe in detail mourning for a most serious occasion. [1]

The final passage of the chapter [2] begins: "Behold days are coming." [3] This formula with "days" often follows predictions beginning "in that day." [4] In such a message conditions are described which are caused by the decision and action "on that day." [5]

Here that which caused the great mourning results in the "word of Jahweh" being heard in the land no more. [6] People who were concerned only with the coming of the fall rains would become aware that "man does not live by bread alone," [7] nor water alone. Though they seek it like the thirsty in a time of drought, it cannot be found. [8]

"Beautiful maidens and young men" [9] perhaps are a play on the participants in the ritual mourning who act out their thirst and swoonings only to be revived when the promise of water and returning rain is heard. But apostate Israelites, worshippers of Ashimah, [10] Dan, [11] and the Way of Beer Sheba [12] will find their favorite oaths and religious formulas of no effect. [13] What was played out in cult drama will be bitter reality without the cult's happy ending. "They shall fall and never rise again." (viii 14).

---

[1] T. MEEK, *Hebrew Origins* (2nd ed., New York, 1950), p. 90; OESTERLEY, *Immortality and the Unseen World* (London, 1921), pp. 101 ff., and 141 ff.; PEDERSEN, *Israel III-IV*, pp. 483 ff.; A. LODS, *Israel* (London, 1932), pp. 218 ff.; SUKENIK, *Memorial Lagrange* (Paris, 1940), pp. 59-65; SCHOFIELD, *S.H.R.*, p. 55; M. DELCOR, *R.B.* LVII (1951), pp. 189-199; *Id., V.T.* III (1953), pp. 67-77.

[2] Amos viii 11-14.

[3] Cf. the discussion in chapter IV.

[4] Amos iii 14 and iv 2; viii 9-10 and 11; ix 11-13.

[5] McCULLOUGH, *op. cit.*, p. 254 observes: "Some of his (Amos') words, however, imply the prospect of a limited activity in the community after the Day has come. (ii 16, iii 12, v 3, 15, 16, vii 17, viii 11-13)."

[6] Amos viii 11d.

[7] Dt. viii 3 and Matt. iv 4.

[8] Amos viii 12.

[9] Amos viii 13. The phrase occurs in a number of other passages: Is. xxiii 4; Jer. xxxi 13; li 22; Sam. i 18; ii 21; etc. The proximity in each of these to the words "daughter" or "virgin daughter" of a nation or city and the constant character of the passages as laments indicates a fixed "Sitz im Leben" that would bear further investigation.

[10] A goddess referred to in the Elephatine Papyri. Cf. SNAITH, *R.R.*, p. 257; S. TALMON, "Notes on the Habakkuk Scroll," *V.T.* I (1951), p. 35.

[11] Cf. Ju. xxii-xxiii and I Kings xxii 26-31.

[12] Often emended to read: "your beloved, Beer Sheba."

[13] This oath was not only a sign of religious allegance and faith, but may reflect cult practice. Cf. W. BAUDISSIN, *op. cit.*, p. 452, n. 2.

What is it that shall cause this inversion of festal rites? this wailing and mourning? Nothing so effectively as "the *End*" which the vision announced. At the moment in which the people would expect to hear the announcement of covenant renewal, the prophetic word was one of rejection, denial—"the End." [1] And if this were accompanied by a sign like an eclipse, the description would have been fulfilled to the letter. [2]

This short exegesis has shown the possibility of treating this chapter as a clearly formed literary unit following a definite pattern. [3] The pattern was this:

1. Vision. viii 1-2.
2. Summary of the ensuing message (a key word). viii 3.
3. Accusation (Indictment of people's sin). viii 4-6.
4. Theological explanation or comment. viii 7-8.
5. "On that day"—God's decision. viii 9-10.
6. "In those days"—results. viii 11-14.

This exegetical study demonstrates that the visionary account is here a very definite part of the chapter and is closely related to the following "words." [4] But can this be traced elsewhere in Amos?

First we should note that the third vision is also followed by such a "word fragment" [5] which summarizes the message arising from the experience recorded in the vision. [6] It is obvious that other "words" growing out of the experience are not to be found in ch. vii except for vs. 17. [7] Where might they be found? The obvious place to look is chs. i-vi.

Following the superscription in ch. i is a cryptic and short "word" similar in many ways to the one in vii 9 and viii 3. It pictures a roar going out from Jahweh which will *wither* fields and the top of

---

[1] Cf. Ez. vii 2-3; Sam. iv 18; Jer. li 13 (of Babylon.)

[2] See vs. 9. If the sign of acceptance was the appearance of the sun's rays in the temple as MORGENSTERN and others have thought, this sign of rejection would have been doubly effective.

[3] In direct contradiction to WEISER, *op. cit.*, p. 249, 258-59; even McCULLOUGH is led to say: "We are driven to the conclusion that the book is a collection of fragments of Amos' speeches." Our investigation rather points to these as small units arranged in an intelligent order everywhere in Amos except perhaps in chs. iii-vi.

[4] I.e. It may not arbitrarily be separated from them as WEISER does.

[5] Amos vii 9.

[6] Amos vii 6-8.

[7] Even the "word" in vs. 17 is strongly conditioned by the conflict with the priest and can only in this secondary sense be related to the vision.

Carmel. [1] The "foreign prophecies" which follow are miniatures of the pattern—Introduction, Accusation, Judgement. [2] They repeat God's judgement by "fire" [3] so often that they remind us of the second vision. [4] Can it be that this is the message growing out of the experience recounted in the second vision?

ii 6-8 presents an accusation like that in viii 4-6. ii 9-12 is a kind of theological explanation like viii 7-8. ii 13 "I will cause to roll under you" is a statement of judgement like that in viii 8-10. ii 14-16— demonstrates the people's helplessness to resist God's judgement in a striking parallel to viii 11-14. Their utter weakness would fit the kind of judgement by "fire" [5] which withered Carmel [6] and which is described in the second vision.

The pattern is here clearly seen again with the foreign prophecies forming a prelude to that against Israel. [7] But a restudy of the vision reveals an element which must be added to the pattern: the prophet's intercession with its result. [8] The vision's description of the progress of the judgement [9] gives the impression of passage of time and leads to the placing of this phase at the end of the list. [10]

---

[1] WEISER, op. cit., p. 265 f. has guessed that this might indicate an earthquake and notes "Eine gewisse Aehnlichkeit mit den Visionen." He goes on to say, "i 2 sollte nach der Absicht seines Verfassers nichts anderes sein, als eine kurze zusammenfassende Umschreibung dessen was in der Visionenreihe gesagt war." It has been suggested that this represented a drought. Cf. RUDOLPH, op. cit., p. 22; WÜRTHWEIN, op. cit., p. 265. But this misses the point and power of vision and speech. Cf. MAAG, Köhler Festschrift, p. 49; STEPHANY, "Charakter und zeitliche Aufeinanderfolge der Drohsprüche in der Profetie des Amos," Christentum und Wissenschaft (1931), p. 288 f.

[2] 1. "For three transgressions . . . I will not turn it back." 2. "Because . . . has done so and so." 3. "I will do so and so."

[2] Amos i 4, 7, 10, 12, 14; ii 2, 5.

[4] Amos vii 4-6, "The Lord Jahweh was calling for a judgement by fire." Cf. RUDOLPH, op. cit., p. 21.

[5] רִיב בָּאֵשׁ perhaps better "an ordeal by fire." Cf. HEMPEL, "Ordal", R.G.G. IV (2nd. ed., 1930), cols. 745-47; PEDERSEN, Israel II-IV, pp. 284 (694-5), 516 (735). Cf. PRESS, "Das Ordal im alten Israel", Z.A.W. 51 (1931), pp. 121-46; 227-55; also Num. xvi-xvii, Korah's ordeal by fire with Moses as intercessor; I Kings xviii with Elijah as intercessor.

[6] Can the reference to Carmel (I Kings xviii) indicate that this was a rite firmly fixed in Carmel's cult?

[7] Amos ii 6-16.

[8] Amos vii 5-6.

[9] The phrase, "I shall not turn it back," seems to be a formula fitted to this theme of judgement by ordeal. It was from even this determined application of the ritual ordeal which the prophet's intercession gained reprieve when it was quite apparent that the people could not stand the test (ii 12-16 and vii 4).

[10] RUDOLPH, op. cit., pp. 21, 25; HÄUSSERMANN, Wortempfang und Symbol, (B.Z.A.W. 58, Giessen, 1932).

The envisioned plague of locusts must certainly have resulted in such prophetic messages. iv 6-13 reviews a series of chastising judgements which failed to turn the people to repentance. But it is obvious that no such "words" are included in our book. [1]

The summary of judgement which follows the third vision pictures defeat by an army [2] and resultant destruction of royal house and sanctuaries. [3] Statements of such a judgement are to be found sprinkled through chs. iii-vi. (iii 11; iii 13-15; vi 8, 11, 14). The results are pictured as exile [4] with its grief. [5] The element of accusation is not lacking [6] while there are abundant passages dealing with theological explanations. [7] These chapters fulfill the requirements of being messages spoken on the basis of the third vision. [8]

There is a new element present in these chapters which belongs in the pattern of prophetic speech and activity. Three times in ch. v the prophet pleads with the people to repent. [9] This along with vision, "word," and intercession are the distinctive tasks of the prophet. In this third period, as in the following two, intercession is forbidden the prophet. [10]

If we turn to ch. ix can we find anything of this pattern? Vss. 1-4 describe something which is more audition than vision in which, however, God is seen [11] already beginning his judgement. [12] Its completeness and inescapableness is emphasized. [13] The last line of the vision [14] (ix 4b) contains what might be called a summary:

---

[1] This clearly indicates the limits of our records of Amos' ministry. He must have worked in a much wider area and period than these records indicate.

[2] Amos vii 9, 17.

[3] Amos vii 9.

[4] Amos iv 2b; v 5; vi 7.

[5] Amos v 16.

[6] Amos iii 9-10, 15; iv 1-3; v 10-12.

[7] Amos iii 2, 3-8, 12; iv 6-13; v 17.

[8] That is, they as fragments fill in nicely the outline like that in ch. viii and remain consistently on the theme summarized in vii 9.

[9] Amos v 4-5 (to the false worshippers); v 14-15 (to the corrupt rich); and v 24 (to the combined people); M. BUBER, *The Prophetic Faith* (N.Y., 1949), p. 106 dates Amos' calls to repentence between his first and last vision, thus supporting our view of the visions running parallel to the words in Amos' ministry.

[10] Amos vii 8d.

[11] Vision is limited to the first line of vs. 1. WEISER, *op. cit.*, p. 263 notes that the location of the vision is uncertain.

[12] This is the force of the imperative preceded by the participle.

[13] "No one of them shall flee away, no one of them shall escape." Note, however, a parallel to the "ordeal formula" of chs. i-ii, "I will not turn it back."

[14] Amos ix 4c.

"I have set my eye upon them for evil and not for good."[1]

There follows in ix 5-10 a theological passage dealing with God's universal control and interest[2] and the idea of a remnant[3] left after sifting the nation in judgement. Destruction is upon the "sinful kingdom."[4] A remnant of the people must somehow be saved.[5]

Then comes an "in that day" passage (ix 11-12) pinning this hope of a remnant to the Davidic house.[6] And finally there is a picture of the coming paradise of "those days" in ix 13-15.[7]

Here, too, is a clear outline like the pattern in ch. viii.[8]

---

[1] Note the tone of an announced decision, like that in viii 3, vii 9, and i 2·

[2] Note the parallels ii 9-12; ii 2.

[3] The judgement of GORDIS, *op. cit.*, p. 250 and others that it is simply patriotic love which accounts for the idea of the "remnant" is certainly far too shallow. Cf. WEISER, *op. cit.*, p. 257. The idea of a remnant is far older than the eighth century prophets. Cf. H. H. ROWLEY, *The Biblical Doctrine of Election* (London, 1950), p. 70.

The idea of a remnant in relation to a ritual of judgement by ordeal as we have pictured it would be a logical necessity.

[4] This can hardly refer to any other than the Northern Kingdom. Cf. V. MAAG, *Text Amos*, p. 250.

[5] McCULLOUGH, *op. cit.*, p. 254 says of vss. ix 8b-15: "in their conviction that Jahweh's ultimate purpose for Israel is good, they are in harmony with the prophet's basic assumptions." These assumptions are those based on election within the covenant.

[6] Recent criticism has tended to return to an acceptance of this passage as genuine. Cf. MAAG, *op. cit.*, p. 62; HAMMERSHAIMB, *Amos* (Copenhagen, 1946), p. 134 ff.

[7] This passage contains familiar features of Israel's "hope" in the 8th century B.C. Amos contributes nothing original in these verses, but there is no reason to doubt that he spoke them.

[8] Outline of the pattern showing relation of visions and words:

	I.	II.	III.	IV.	V.	Biograp
Vision	vii 1	vii 4	vii 7-8	viii 1-2a	ix 1-4	(vii 7-8)
Key Word	—	i 2	vii 9	viii 3	ix 4b	(vii 9)
Accusation (application)	—	ii 6-8	iii 9-10, 15 / iv 1-3 / v 10-12	viii 4-6	—	vii 10-1
Theological Explanation (rationalization)	—	ii 9-12	iii 2, 3-8, 12 / iv 6-13 / v 17b	viii 7-8	ix 5-8	vii 14-1
God's Decision "On that day"	—	ii 13	iii 11, 13-15 / vi 8, 11, 14	viii 9-10	ix 11-12	—
Results "In those days"	—	ii 14-16	iv 2-3 / v 5, 16 / vi 7	viii 11-14	ix 13-15	vii 17
Pleas for Repentance	—	—	v 4-5, 14-15, 24	—	—	
Intercession and Result	vii 2-3	vii 5-6	vii 8b / Not allowed	viii 2b / Not allowed	—	—

It may be noted in passing that even the biographic account follows this scheme: vision, key word (vs. 9), basis for judgement (vs. 10-13), theological explanation (vss. 14-16), prophecy of judgement (vs. 17).

There is, then, a definite progression shown by the visions and their associated words. [1] The first two visions announce a kind of trial by ordeal [2] from which a reprieve is granted although it is obvious that Israel was not able to stand the test. [3] It is equally clear that Israel was not moved to repentance. [4] Then God announced that he himself was setting up a trial in the midst of his people. [5] The results of this trial were simply proved guilt and continued unrepentance which called for judgement by the sword, the fall of the reigning house, and widespread destruction including mansions and sanctuaries. [6] Also the prophet is forbidden to intercede. The judgement is final. The fourth announces the End of covenant relations. [7] While the fifth envisions punishment as already beginning, it renews the promise of completeness, and turns to the question of "after that, what?"

It is quite clear, then, that all of the messages in Amos do not come after this last vision. [8] Certainly the pleas to Israel to repent [9] should come before the complete end of covenant relations is announced.

The visions are much better understood then as recording critical turning points in the ministry of Amos. [10] They give him the basic understanding of God's purposes which makes possible his presentation of the various messages then given to him. Together they give an account of the full span of Amos' recorded ministry, and therefore cannot be placed before his call. [11] All five were probably spoken

---

[1] RUDOLPH, *op. cit.*, p. 24.

[2] What BRIGHT, *The Kingdom of God* (New York, 1953), p. 88 calls a "discipline" and R. de VAUX, *R.B.* XLIII (1933), p. 528 calls "chastisement."

[3] The nature of the ordeals might indicate that their purpose was not to be a real test but to demonstrate Israel's lack of righteousness and her need for a saviour.

[4] Amos based his plea for forgiveness on Israel's weakness (i.e. God's grace) rather than on a change in Israel's attitude.

[5] Amos vii 8.

[6] Amos vii 9.

[7] The end of Israel's status as God's people (viii 2b).

[8] WEISER, *op. cit.*, p. 263 to the contrary. Cf. literature given by CRIPPS, *op. cit.*, p. 101, n. 4.

[9] In ch. v.

[10] Not as those steps leading up to his call. Cf. RUDOLPH, *op. cit.*, p. 25.

[11] As WEISER and RUDOLPH do.

together on the occasion of the last one, but the others may have been spoken earlier in groups of three and four.

D. THE TWO BOOKS OF AMOS

It is correct to think of "two books of Amos." [1] But they do not represent simply two literary forms, as Weiser suggested. The Bethel story tells us why there had to be two books. Amos' ministry in the Northern Kingdom was interrupted before God had finished speaking his message concerning Israel. The visions, words, and biographical section of the last three chapters were gathered by adherents, friends, or fellow prophets at some southern sanctuary. [2] This might well be called a "Book of Visions" for they form its distinctive feature. But this book contains "words" and biography as well.

The "words" found in chs. i-vi, on the other hand, were spoken in the North, were remembered, repeated, and copied down there. They must have found their way into the South along with other refugees [3] and finally been united with the other Book of Amos to form our present book. [4]

"Vision" and "word" belong together. The prophet's message cannot be understood apart from those great moments when God revealed his counsel [5] and the prophet was allowed to see eternal meaning in temporal appearance. Thus both "word" and "vision" gain in depth and coherence. Amos has always been reckoned a giant among men of God. He was a man who "saw" God's truth and unhesitatingly spoke God's word.

---

[1] See above p. 27.

[2] H. J. KRAUS, *Gottesdienst in Israel*, p. 116 suggests that the reason Israel preserved the prophets' words was because they represented a charismatic realization of God's law, of revelation. The recent study by SOSUMU JOZAKI, *The Secondary Passages of the Book of Amos* (Kwansei Gakuin University Annual Studies IV; Nishinomiya, Japan, 1956) has not been available to me.

[3] Like Hosea and Deuteronomy: KRAUS, *op. cit.*, pp. 94-5.

[4] This final process could have occurred at any time between the fall of the northern kingdom and the completion of the scroll of the Twelve Prophets well after the Exile. But the works so joined are to be viewed as the authentic works of Amos. Cf. GORDIS, *op. cit.*, p. 251; EVA OSSWALD, *Urform und Auslegung im masoretischen Amos Text: ein Beitrag zur Kritik an der neueren traditionsgeschichtlichen Methode* (diss. Jena, 1951) cf. *T.L.Z.* 80 (1955), col. 179.

[5] Amos iii 7.

CHAPTER THREE

AN OLD HYMN PRESERVED IN THE
BOOK OF AMOS [1]

A number of scholars have recently drawn attention to passages in the Book of Amos which display hymnic form. [2] They are found in iv 13, v 8, and ix 5-6. [3] It is the purpose of this chapter to analyse these hymnic portions, define their limits, [4] and determine their relation to each other before turning to other observations concerning their presence in the book of Amos.

---

[1] The first part of this chapter appeared originally in *J.N.E.S.* XV (1956), pp. 33-39 and is used again with the consent of the editor.

[2] H. SCHMIDT, *Der Prophet Amos* (Tübingen, 1917), p. 23, n. 1; K. BUDDE, "Zu Text und Auslegung des Buches Amos", *J.B.L.* XLIV (1925), p. 106; F. HORST, "Die Doxologien im Amosbuch, "*Z.A.W.* XLVII (1929), pp. 45-54; H. GUNKEL, *Einleitung in die Psalmen* (Göttingen, 1933), p. 33; T. H. GASTER, "An Ancient Hymn in the Prophecies of Amos", *J.M.E.O.S.* XIX (1935), pp. 23-26; E. HAMMERSHAIMB, *Amos* (Copenhagen, 1946), pp. 72, 79, and 132; A. WEISER, *Das Buch der zwölf kleinen Propheten* I (*A.T.D.* XXIV, Göttingen, 1949), p. 135; V. MAAG, *Text, Wortschatz und Begriffswelt des Buches Amos* (hereafter *Text Amos*) (Leiden, 1951), pp. 24 and 56 ff.; W. S. McCULLOUGH, "Some Suggestions about Amos", *J.B.L.* LXXII (1953), p. 248.

[3] BUDDE, HORST, and MAAG limit the hymn of these verses. GASTER includes v 9, while SCHMIDT includes iv 12b-c.

[4] Many attempts at reconstruction can be cited. BUDDE saw the hymn as a single whole. HORST understood it as comprising two strophes of four 3-3 lines each. SCHMIDT thinks of three strophes composed of two 3-3 lines with prologue and refrain for each. GASTER reconstructed three strophes, each with a refrain, plus a fragment of the fourth in v 9. V. MAAG, *Festschrift für Ludwig Köhler*, *S.T.U.* xx (1950), p. 46, writes of four strophes composed of two 3-3 lines each.

Other scholars have understood the lines to be integral parts of the text composed by Amos. K. CRAMER, *Amos* (Stuttgart, 1930), p. 90, says each hymnic portion belongs so closely to its context that it can not be lifted out. McCULLOUGH follows him in stressing that these are genuine to the speeches of Amos. This insight does not necessarily answer the question concerning the origin of the hymn. Amos may very well have spoken the words and yet have been quoting familiar fragments of a current hymn.

D. GUTHE, "Amos", *Die Heilige Schrift des alten Testaments*, ed. E. KAUTZSCH (Tübingen, 1923) II, p. 37, suggests that these doxologies marked the end of various collections of prophecies as in the Psalms, but he has found little support from other writers.

A. THE FIRST HYMN FRAGMENT

The first passage is usually recognized in iv 13. Participles characteristic of hymnic measure [1] are found here with a highly formal
refain: "Jahweh God of Hosts is His name." But careful study shows
that this verse is very closely related to vs. 12. "Prepare to meet thy
God, Israel!" leads up very nicely to the doxology found in vs. 13.
There seems to be no good reason for separating the two verses. [2]

There is, however, an excellent reason for questioning the unity
of vs. 12. One complete clause appears in duplicate: "Therefore
thus shall I do to you, Israel. Because I shall do this to you Israel,
prepare . . . ." The first of these clearly brings the Jahweh word of
Amos to its climax, [3] while the second rephrases it making the
transition to what follows. The whole may very well have been
used by the prophet in this way, [4] but the cumbersome transition
nevertheless reveals that the whole was not a single composition. [5]
Rather the latter appears to be a quotation which was used to support
the prophet's point. [6]

The last part of vs. 12, this imperative call to assembled Israel,
belongs to the quotation. Such an imperative is a common characteristic of Hebrew hymns [7] and is therefore quite an appropriate
element of the hymnic portion. The quotation does not extend
beyond vs. 13, for chap. v begins with a very different theme. This
quoted hymn strophe reads then as follows:

iv 12c   הִכּוֹן לִקְרַאת אֱלֹהֶיךָ יִשְׂרָאֵל   4 [8]

---

[1] GUNKEL, *op. cit.*, pp. 44-45; HORST, *op. cit.*, p. 46.

[1] CRAMER, *op. cit.*

[3] This is precisely CRAMER's argument.

[4] In full agreement with CRAMER, MAAG, and McCULLOUGH at this point.

[5] As the studies, listed above, indicate.

[6] MAAG, *op. cit.*, and others.

[7] GUNKEL, *op. cit.*, p. 43.

[8] E. BALLA, "Ezechiel viii 1-9, 11; xi 24-25", *Bultmann Festschrift* (Stuttgart,
1949), p. 1 ff.; G. FOHRER, "Jeremias Tempelwort vii 1-15", *Theologische Zeit-
schrift* V (1949), p. 401 ff.; FOHRER, "Berichte über symbolische Handlungen
der Propheten", *Z.A.W.* LXIV (1952), p. 105 ff.; FOHRER, *Die Haupt-
probleme des Buches Ezechiel* (*B.Z.A.W.* LXXII, Berlin, 1952), p. 63 ff.; FOHRER,
"Über den Kurzvers", *Z.A.W.* LXVI (1954), p. 199 ff., have argued for the
existence of such lines in Hebrew poetry against S. MOWINCKEL, "Der metrische
Aufbau von Jes. lxii 1-12 und der neue sogenannte 'Kurzvers' ", *Z.A.W.* LXV
(1953), pp. 167-87; and T. H. ROBINSON, "Hebrew Poetic Form: the English
Tradition", *Supplements to Vetus Testamentum* I, *Congress Volume* (1953), p. 139 ff.
The only possible division of this line into two parts would have to be a 3-1
combination which would hardly be acceptable to these latter writers. This

2-2-3   iv 13   יוֹצֵר הָרִים וּבֹרֵא רוּחַ ² וּמַגִּיד לְאָדָם מַה־שֵּׂחוֹ !

3-3   עֹשֵׂה שַׁחַר ³ עֵיפָה וְדֹרֵךְ עַל־בָּמֳתֵי אָרֶץ

4   יַהְוֶה אֱלֹהֵי צְבָאוֹת שְׁמוֹ

iv 12c   Prepare to meet your God, Israel!
iv 13   Former of mountains
         Creator of wind [4]
             One revealing to man what His thought is
         Making dawn of darkness
         And treading upon the heights of the earth
         Is He whose [5] name is Jahweh God of Hosts.

The strophe is interesting in many ways. It seems to form a complete whole from its imperative introduction which calls upon Israel to prepare to encounter her God, through the participial descriptions of him, to the refrain which in festal emphasis pronounces his name. The measure is common. Only the second line with its tristich measure of 2-2-3 [6] calls for special notice.

The theme of the verse centers in "Jahweh God of Hosts" [7] whom Israel is about to meet. The verse sings praise of him as Creator and

---

forces us back to the conclusion that there is here an opening and closing line for this strophe made of a single unit of four accents.

[1] In this reconstruction the two particles כִּי הִנֵּה are left out. They may be considered an expansion of the original by the prophet as he quotes (MAAG, *Text Amos*, p. 24) or they may be considered a kind of anacrusis like that which T. H. ROBINSON, "Anacrusis in Hebrew Poetry", *Werden und Wesen des Alten Testaments B.Z.A.W.* LXVI (1936), p. 37 ff., thought of. For the original hymn they are unnecessary and may best be omitted.

[2] HORST, *op. cit.*, p. 49, emends the text so as to be translated. "Who freely grants to men whatever they need." GASTER, *op. cit.*, pp. 24-25 emends the phrase to read, "And maketh her foison to grow unto the earth." But the verse makes perfectly good sense in stating that God through his creation reveals his intentions and purposes.

[3] HORST, *op. cit.*, is reminded of the Accadian creation myth in which the storm wind overcomes Tiamat. The hymn's emphasis is in sharp contrast to that mythical conception.

[4] This rendering understands this last clause as a contact relative clause which has its relation to the previous sentence defined by the final pronominal suffix. See L. KÖHLER, "שָׁאַד יָשׁוּב und der nackte Relativsatz", *V.T.* III (1953), pp. 84-85.

[5] HORST, *op. cit.*, p. 49, and MAAG, *op. cit.*, p. 24, follow the Septuagint in adding a conjunction. But the Massoretic rendering makes good sense while keeping the poetic phrase terse and poignant. For the meaning of עֵיפָה see L. KÖHLER, "Die Morgenröte im A.T.", *Z.A.W.* XLIV (1926), pp. 56-59.

[6] Cf. TH. H. ROBINSON, "Principles of Hebrew Poetic Form", *B.F.*, p. 448.

[7] CRAMER, *op. cit.*, p. 95, relates iv 13 to i 3ff. and thus emphasizes this fact.

Lord of creation. This theme is significant enough when we consider that the hymn must be older than Amos. [1] But we should note the added element: God reveals his "thoughts to man," evidently through his creation. [2]

It has been suggested that "Hosts" indicate the various powers known to the ancient world, demons dwelling in mountains and wind, in dawn and darkness, and that the verse, like the Name which crowns it, sings Jahweh's authority and power over all of them. [3] The theme of Jahweh's authority and greatness is sung in terms of creation and its control by nature's triumphant Lord. Such is Israel's God whom she must prepare to meet.

B.   THE SECOND HYMN FRAGMENT

The second passage is in v 8. This verse is also in typical hymnic form with prominent participles. The first line is composed of three elements of three accents each [4] characterizing God's control of heavenly bodies and the sequence of day and night. The second line has two three-accent elements telling his control of the rain. At the end is the short refrain familiar from iv 13, but here in a shortened form: "Jahweh is his name."

Again we must seek the limits of the hymn. The Massoretic rendering of vs. 7 is anything but hymnic and seems out of context here. I have suggested elsewhere [5] that the verse should be read with a singular subject following the Septuagint. When this is done, it naturally forms a very intimate part of the hymn. [6] The previous verse (6), like iv 12c, is an imperative which is quite at home in a

---

[1] HORST, op. cit., p. 49, quite rightly compares this verse to Ps. lxv 7 ff.

[2] MAAG's comment, Köhler Festschrift, p. 47, is to the point: "This verse has nothing to do with God's creative acts. Rather he maintains that it is Jahweh who delivers oracles and truth so that no conjured spirits are necessary. The entire hymn points out that Jahweh rules the world from the granting of oracles to the course of the stars."

[3] Ibid., p. 48: "Is it not clear what conception for the poet lay behind the expression ṣebaoth? They are the legions of powers who functioned in the lower religions, spirits who pulled the wind, gleamed in the dawn, who had once piled the mountains on each other in order to house mountain spirits in them, who were active within the earth and caused earthquakes, whose uncanny play cast spring floods over the land," and so without end. "Instead of these for the poet only Jahweh reigns—so he is called God of Hosts." Cf. also WAMBACQ, L'Epithète Divine Jahwé Sebaôt (de Brouer, 1947).

[4] ROBINSON, op. cit.

[5] "Note on the Text of Amos v 7", V.T. IV (1954), p. 215.

[6] As CRAMER, op. cit., p. 94, has noted while rejecting the reading.

hymnic setting. But the passage cannot be traced further back for there is again a clear duplication between vss. 4*b*-5 and vs. 6. The former is in the first person and forms the climax of vss. 1-5. Vs. 6 is in the third person repeating the phrase. It may be argued that this is simply the statement in the prophet's own words on the basis of Jahweh's words which preceded. [1] But it is more likely that the Jahweh word ended with a play on a familiar hymn which is now documented through inclusion in the Book of Amos by the compiler, be he the prophet or another. [2]

Vs. 9 seems also to belong to the hymn although the reading of the present Hebrew text is uncertain. [3] The suggested reading of HOFFMANN, [4] however, gives the sense of God's control of heavenly constellations in perfect parallelism to the first line of vs. 8. With this reading it should certainly be counted a part of the hymn which cannot extend beyond vs. 9. The following verse picks up the accusations directed toward sinful Israelites. This being true, the refrain in vs. 8 would certainly have to be put after vs. 9. [5]

One other question remains to be answered. The second line of vs. 8 concerning Jahweh's control of rain is duplicated in ix 6. In the latter place it fits quite snugly. In chap. v it separates two lines dealing with heavenly bodies. Its position in the original hymn is therefore best found in ix 6 and omitted from v 8. [6]

This strophe of a hymn in v 6-9 may then be read thus:

---

[1] As CRAMER, *op. cit.*, p. 93, has done.

[2] A. WEISER, *Die Prophetie des Amos*, B.Z.A.W. LIII (1929), p. 183 ff., has clearly shown the break between these two verses which MAAG's criticism, *Text Amos*, pp. 28-29, does not fully refute.

[3] GASTER, *op. cit.*, has attempted an emendation which he translates: "He who maketh destruction to come upon men's strongholds, and bringeth ruin on their fortress."

[4] Z.A.W. III (1883), pp. 110-11; G. R. DRIVER, "Two Astronomical Passages in the Old Testament", *J.T.S.* IV (1953), pp. 208-12; MAAG, *Köhler Festschrift*, pp. 46-47, n. 4, notes that part of vs. 8 has been lost which must have had something to do with movements of the stars. Although the meter suggested here is quite different from MAAG's, his surmise seems correct. Vs. 9 in HOFFMAN's emendation supplies that line having to do with star movements. WEISER, *op. cit.*, p. 203, argues against HOFFMAN's view. But he has missed the point that the second half of verse 8 is a duplicate of ix 5 and does not belong here at all.

[5] DRIVER, *op. cit.*, p. 209.

[6] GASTER, *op. cit.*, p. 24, holds that the original position of this line is in v 8. But this arrangement of the lines shows that the strophe is a unit when this is left out and vs. 9 (as emended) read in its place.

3-2-2   דִּרְשׁוּ אֶת־יַהְוֶה וִחְיוּ פֶּן־יִצְלַח כָּאֵשׁ ¹ וְאָכְלָה וְאֵין־מְכַבֶּה ²   v 6

4-3   ³ יַהְוֶה פִּכֶּה מִלְמַעֲלָה מִשְׁפָּם וּצְדָקָה לָאֶרֶץ הִגִּיחַ   v 7

3-3-3   ⁴ עֹשֶׂה כִימָה וּכְסִיל וְהֹפֵךְ לַבֹּקֶר צַלְמָוֶת וְיוֹם לַיְלָה הֶחְשִׁיךְ   v 8

3-3-2   ⁵ הַמַּבְלִיג שֹׁר עַל־עָז וְשֹׁר עַל־מִבְצָר יָבוֹא ⁶ יַהְוֶה שְׁמוֹ   v 9

v 6   Seek Jahweh and live!
　　　Lest He break out like fire
　　　Which consumes beyond quenching.
v 7   Jahweh (it is who) caused justice to trickle down from above
　　　And established righteousness for the earth, ⁶
v 8   Making Pleiades and Orion ⁷
　　　Turning deep darkness to morning,
　　　Who darkened day into night.
v 9   The One causing Taurus to vanquish ⁸ Capella
　　　And who will cause Taurus to set upon Vindemiatrix
　　　Is He whose name is Jahweh.

Here again is a compact strophe of four lines. The first line is an inverted 7 in three parts: 3-2-2. ⁹ The second is an ordinary 7 with 4 and 3. The third is a line of nine in three parts, while the fourth has eight accents in three parts including the two-beat refrain.

This time the name Jahweh appears in the first line in a call to seek him and in him seek life. The threat of judgement (or ordeal) by fire is posed in the latter parts of the first line, reminding one of Amos' second vision.¹⁰ In this setting the second line's justice and

---

¹ ² The two phrases emphasizing the application of the message to Israel do not fit the meter and can hardly have been a part of the original hymn. Their appearance in the text is easily explained as an attempt to make explicit what is implicit in the hymn.
³ See p. 54 n. 5.
⁴ See p. 55 n. 6.
⁵ See p. 55 n. 4.
⁶ See p. 55 n. 5.
⁷ Cf. S. MOWINCKEL, "Die Sternennamen im Alten Testament", N.T.T. XXIX (1928), p. 5.
⁸ S. GRÜNBERG, Jahrbuch der jüdisch-literarischen Gesellschaft XIX (1928), pp. 279-92, suggests that the hiphil stem of בלג is equivalent to the Arabic (IV) פלג, and means "siegen lassen".
⁹ S. MOWINCKEL, "Zum Problem der hebräischen Metrik", B.F., p. 392, has expressed his doubts that a three phase verse foot exists in Hebrew. However, ROBINSON, op. cit., p. 148; ROBINSON, B.F., p. 448; and F. HORST, "Die Kennzeichen der hebräischen Poesie", T.R. XXI (1953), p. 109, seem to sum up the consensus of most scholars in agreeing that such three part lines do exist in various combinations, three of which are illustrated in this strophe.
¹⁰ MAAG, Köhler Festschrift, p. 49, reminds us that this mythical fire belongs always in Amos inseparably with Jahweh.

righteousness seem to have no reference to social ethics, but to the divine order in nature. The judgment taking place involves the courses of nature, and it is Jahweh himself who has ordained just and righteous measures "for the earth."

The final two lines tell of Jahweh's control of the movements of stars and constellations and through them of days, months, and seasons. Vs. 9 particularly portrays a time before Taurus has set and Vindemiatrix has risen. [1]

This latter points to the time of the autumnal New Year. The themes of "seeking Jahweh," of life, of judgment, of nature's ordinances, of light and dark, of the change of seasons, and of the mysteries revealed by the stars are fitly related to that season.

The call of the previous strophe is taken a step further. Preparation requires seeking Jahweh in face of judgment and recognizing in him the omnipotent Lord of fate [2] as well as the universe. The particular stars mentioned are familiar to students of folklore and mythology. The point of the hymn is to stress Jahweh's complete control of all those cosmic elements which were often held to possess separate powers affecting the lives and well-being of the peoples.

C. THE THIRD HYMN FRAGMENT

The final passage is found in ix 5-6. Its limits are more clearly recognized by all. Here again is the phenomenon of duplication. ix 5*b* is a duplicate of viii 8*b*. The evidence that Amos in viii 8*b* makes a word play on a familiar hymn is clear. [3] The original in hymnic setting appears in ix 5*b*. [4]

The second duplication appears in ix 6*b* and v 8*c*. This was noted above where it was observed that the proper setting in the hymn is in this later passage.

These duplications do not connect the words of the hymn with those of Amos like the earlier instances. They rather show the relation of two fragments to each other. Evidently the fragment in chap. v and that in chap. ix are from the same hymn so that in quoting one line might be used in two places.

---

[1] DRIVER, *op. cit.*

[2] H. GROSS, *Weltherrschaft als religiöse Idee im Alten Testament* (*B.B.B.* VI, Bonn, 1953), contends that the concept of Jahweh's control of the fate of all is the seed idea of God's lordship and of eschatology.

[3] MAAG, *Text Amos*, p. 53.

[4] MAAG, *Köhler Festschrift*, p. 46, n. 4. Although BUDDE, *op. cit.*, p. 107, argues that the duplicate is original to viii 8 and does not belong to the doxology.

Some might think that the formal name of Jahweh is not fitting for an introduction to a verse, but when the three strophes are seen together this can hardly be maintained. The first strophe only reveals the "name" at the end. The second has it in the first line as object of an imperative, while this last begins with it as subject. This builds a deliberate climax.

But a peculiar orthography raises a question about this address. Translated literally, it reads: "Lord Jahweh of the Hosts." It is grammatically questionable whether Jahweh can be read as a construct. [1] Further the technical term would hardly have the article. [2] It is at least permissible then to suggest that there is a mistake, and that the words should be divided differently reading הצבא אותות [3] instead of הצבאות. This should be translated "Lord Jahweh is the one summoning signs." The signs so indicated would be the heavenly signs of the coming change of seasons stressed in the previous strophe.

Another orthographical difficulty occurs near the end of the second line where the Massoretic text has a plural construct noun followed by a preposition: a grammatically impossible construction. The obvious change required is simply the addition of a feminine pronominal suffix. [4]

Vs. 6 begins with a line which has seldom been questioned, but which introduces in its usual translation elements foreign to the themes in vss. 5 and 6*b*. הַבּוֹנֶה, "the one building," adds little to the meaning of the coming season. A slight orthographical change yields מִתְבּוֹנֵן, "the[5] one thinking" or "determining."

In the center of the line is a strange word, וַאֲגֻדָּתוֹ, which is a *hapax legomenon* in such a usage. If the word is divided in two, yielding הוּא גְדָתוֹ, [6] we have a pronoun to be read with the first element of

---

[1] GESENIUS-KAUTZSCH, *Hebrew Grammar* (2nd American ed., Boston, 1893), p. 372. Proper nouns may never be in construct state.

[2] There is no parallel for this usage in the Old Testament. Cf. L. KÖHLER, *Theologie des Alten Testaments* (2nd ed., Tübingen, 1953), p. 32.

[3] This seems to be a case of double haplography.

[4] Assuming again a case of haplography where two words have such similar endings.

[5] The *mem* having dropped out because of similarity to the last letter of the previous word.

[6] Again a case of haplography because of similarity to the last letters of the previous word Cf. KÖHLER-BAUMGARTNER, *Lexicon in Veteris Testamenti Libros*, p. 169.

the line and a noun meaning "his good fortune" [1] or "his bounty"
which approaches the Septuagint's translation τὴν ἐπαγγελίαν.

The strophe of four long lines may be rendered as follows:

ix 5   2-2-3   ² וַאדֹנָי יַהְוֶה ³ הַצֹּבֵא אוֹתוֹת הַנּוֹגֵעַ בָּאָרֶץ וַתִּמּוֹג

3-3-3   וְאָבְלוּ כָּל־יוֹשְׁבֵיהָ ⁴ בָהּ וְעָלְתָה כַיְאֹר כֻּלָּה וְשָׁקְעָה כִּיאֹר מִצְרָיִם

ix 6   4-4   ⁵ מְתַבּוֹנֵן בַּשָּׁמַיִם מַעֲלוֹתוֹ הוּא ⁶ גֻדָּתוֹ עַל־אֶרֶץ יְסָדָהּ

3-3-2   הַקֹּרֵא לְמֵי הַיָּם וַיִּשְׁפְּכֵם עַל פְּנֵי הָאָרֶץ יַהְוֶה שְׁמוֹ

ix 5   Lord Jahweh
          The One summoning signs
             Is the One touching the earth so it will quiver, [7]
          Though all its inhabitants mourn with it
             And its reservoirs [8] rise like the Nile
                And irrigate [9] like the Nile of Egypt.
ix 6   One determining his thoughts (works) [10] in the heavens is He,
             His bounty which he will establish on the earth.
          The One calling to the sea's water
             That he might pour it over the earth's surface
                Is He whose name is Jahweh.

This strophe picks up the references to Jahweh's cosmic control
in order to apply it to the anticipated turn of the seasons. His control

---

[1] It is true that this reading would give the only extent form of גדה in Hebrew
as a feminine. But there are enough parallels in cognate languages to make the
meaning quite clear.

[2] HORST, op. cit., p. 54, refers to J. PEDERSEN, Der Eid bei den Semiten (1914),
p. 16 and calls this "die Schwurpartikel" used with the festal name of God.

[3] Emended on the assumption of double haplography.

[4] Emended to correct haplography. See p. 58.

[5] Restoring a mem. See p. 58.

[6] Words divided differently from M. T. plus letters restored. See p. 58.

[7] The context makes clear that this does not refer to an earthquake but to
the response of the fertile earth to the change of seasons and coming rain. W.
RIEDEL, Alttestamentliche Untersuchungen (Leipzig, 1902), p. 33, attempts an
emendation that will fit the interpretation of an earthquake. But this is wholly
unnecessary in light of the context.

[8] The word is understood to mean an utensil and to refer to the containers
of water used in seasonal rites, perhaps as a kind of sympathetic magic, accompanying prayers for the coming of rain. Cf. Elijah's barrels of water (I Kings
xviii 30 f.); J. PEDERSEN, Israel III-IV (Copenhagen, 1940), p. 750.

[9] For this translation and interpretation see T. H. GASTER, Thespis (New
York, 1950), p. 123.

[10] This translation is based on the analogy of Ezek. xi 5. It might be translated
"his risings up" or "its risings" (this latter referring to the coming of the rains
or to the following floods). GASTER's emendation of "heaven" to read "waters"
(J.M.E.O.S. XIX, p. 25) ignores the fact that the two points of emphasis throughout the hymn are exactly the heavens and the earth.

is not remote. As he calls for the heavenly signs, so it is his touch which awakens the earth to new life. No matter how many ritual observances there be, it is He, not they, which effect the renewal of nature's life. [1]

He is the Lord of all. His decisions are sealed in heaven beyond the influence of earthly ritual, and He himself will carry them out. It is He who calls for water from the sea to slake earth's thirst, [2] none other than Jahweh.

The emphasis and direction of the hymn is obvious. No room is left for the recognition of an intermediate being acting in Jahweh's service. He himself is not only supreme Lord, but He is the only supernatural power controlling all these things. This is radical Jahwism in the clearest expression possible, denying the existence or power of all the forces known to Canaanite and kindred religions. Jahweh stands supreme and alone, independent of ritual, [3] gracious in intent, revealing his purposes to men, demanding only to be honestly sought in worship, but prepared to wreak awful judgment upon those refusing his invitation. All this is what the singer understood by the name, "Jahweh God of Hosts."

D. THE HYMN'S "SITZ IM LEBEN"

In seeking to determine the setting in which the hymn was sung its basic themes must be kept in mind. A setting should be found which adequately explains their presence in the hymn. These themes are:

1) Expectancy of Jahweh's coming (iv 12c). [4]
2) Possibility of judgement or trial by ordeal (v 6). [5]
3) Praise of the Creator (iv 13) [6]

---

[1] MAAG, *Köhler Festschrift*, p. 48, reminds us that the three elements of the Canaanite world picture are included here: heaven, earth, and water.

[2] HORST, *Z.A.W.* XLVII (1929), p. 47, comments: "Jahweh calls the sea's water up to heaven in order to dispense it from there over the earth as rain."

[3] Note the parallel emphasis of the eighth-century prophets.

[4] S. MOWINCKEL, *Religion und Kultus*, p. 76ff.

[5] M. BUBER, *The Prophetic Faith*, p. 106: K. CRAMER, *Amos*, p. 96 thinks of Isaiah ii 10 ff. as being dependent upon Amos. But their similarity is much more easily explained when attributed to a similar background of cultic judgement.

[6] O. EISSFELDT, "Gott und das Meer in der Bibel," *Studia Orientalia Ioanni Pedersen* (Copenhagen, 1953), pp. 76-84 has pointed out that two views of creation are to be found in the Bible. In one the sea is an active opponent of God. In the other it is a docile created servant of God. This hymn belongs to the latter category, while great creation hymns like Ps. civ have many elements of the former.

4) Praise of the Lord of nature (iv 13, v 7-9, ix 5-6) [1]
5) Expectancy of rain (v 9, ix 5-6) [2]
6) Omen of fate (iv 13, v 9, ix 5a and 6a). [3]

The theme of Jahweh's coming and his judgement as well as the expected announcement of what the New Year will bring fit most naturally into the Autumn Festival (later called the Feast of Tabernacles). In this festival which is thought by some to be one of covenant renewal [4] and by others to be an enthronement festival [5] these themes would be quite at home. The climax of the festival was the "Day of Jahweh" [6] on which he appeared, judged, and in assurances of covenant renewal laid the basis for blessing throughout the ensueing year.

This festival fell at the time of the fall equinox [7] when the dry summer season was expected to give way to autumnal rains. Therefore the subject of rain and the promise of renewed fertility in the fields was of general interest. Being the New Year, [8] celebrated simultaneously with nature's renewal, it was the natural season for celebration and teaching about creation and the control of nature. [9] It was a season of change, and the changing patterns of the heavens revealed the coming change of seasons. [10]

It was a time of expectancy as the hymn shows. The rains were eagerly awaited. The crowds anxiously anticipated every phenomenon

---

[1] Cf. Jer. x 13; Ps. cxlvii 16 f. H. W. ROBINSON, *Inspiration and Revelation in the Old Testament* (Oxford, 1946), p. 17 ff. has rightly emphasized the close relation of creation and conservation. We list them here separately to emphasize the fact that both are present.

[2] Ps. lxxii 6; Ps. cxxxv 7; Ps. cxlvii 8; Ps. cxv 9-10; I Kings xvii-xviii; Jer. v 24; x 13; li 16; Hos. vi 3; Joel ii 23; Zech. x 1; Dt. xxviii 12, 24; Isa. xxx 23.

[3] Cf. HEMPEL, "Wort Gottes und Schicksal," *B.F.*, p. 232: "Das Schicksal ist Auswirkung menschlicher Schuld, die menschliche Schuld ist "dämonisches" Schicksal, die Überwindung menschlicher Schuld aber "göttliches" Schicksal—das Gotteswort gestaltet das Schicksal und wird selbst zum Schicksal, zum Gericht wie zur Erlösung."

[4] See p. 72 n. 1.

[5] See p. 38 n. 5.

[6] See following chapter.

[7] GASTER, *Thespis*, p. 30 ff. and p. 340; M. NOTH, *Die Welt des Alten Testaments* (2nd. ed. Berlin, 1953), p. 24.

[8] A. JOHNSON, *Sacral Kingship in Ancient Israel*, pp. 51-4.

[9] *Ibid.*, p. 84; MOWINCKEL, *op. cit.*, p. 75.

[10] G. H. GILMORE, "Stars," *The New Schaff-Herzog Encyclopedia of Religious Knowledge* XI (N.Y., 1911), p. 67; *Encyclopedia Britannica* Vol. 22 (Chicago, 1948), p. 227 explains the use of "star catalogues" for this purpose "going back continuously to . . . 150 B.C. *and earlier*."

which migth be considered an omen of what the future held. [1] The
faithful waited fearfully for the moment when Jahweh would meet
his people. [2]

Some have thought that the entire night preceding the great day
was spent in watching, [3] that the temples oriented toward the East
were situated so as to catch the first rays of the sun which would
foretell a day of "light" and blessing. [4]

It was to a congregation gripped by this contageous expectancy
that this hymn was sung. As they awaited the dawning of that day,
the quiet night making everyone conscious of nature near all around,
the hymn reminded all that Jahweh made and controls these. As
they sniffed the air for signs of moisture heralding the coming rain,
the hymn forced attention to the central issue: "Prepare to meet
your God, Israel!" As the night sky made the stars seem so close as
to be fellow worshippers in the sanctuary court, the hymn sang of
their creator and Lord. As the people whispered the latest rumored
omen for "the Day," the hymn proclaimed Jahweh's control of
fortune and fate. He it is that determines blessing or curse, and his
judgements lie beyond the influence of ritual or magic.

It is worth noting that the use of the tenses support this understanding of the background of the hymn. The time viewpoint [5] of
the hymn is set by the participles and imperatives. The people are
challenged to prepare for an experience that is imminent. The
participles use the immediate observation of things existing (mountains, winds, revelation iv 13, the planets and constellations in the
night sky v 8-9, ix 5a, the time of fall equinox which is at hand
ix 5-6) to demonstrate God's acts. Imperfects point out possible or
expected results of these things (judgement by fire v 6, the expected
setting of Taurus v 9, the expected renewal of nature ix 5, the expected
good omen for the New Year iv 6a, the expected coming of rain
ix 6b). From the hymn's present standpoint all these look forward.
Perfects with *waw* present parallel occurences (the ritual ix 5) or a
subordinate clause (the description of fire v 6). Perfects standing
alone look back from this standpoint in the present to actions

---

[1] H. GRESSMANN, "Astralreligion im Alten Testament," *R.G.G.* I (2nd ed.),
col. 593; A. BERTHOLET, "Omen", *R.G.G.* IV (2nd ed.), cols. 697-9.

[2] MOWINCKEL, *op. cit.*, p. 76.

[3] JOHNSON, *op. cit.*, p. 83. Cf. Jubilees xii 16.

[4] MOWINCKEL, *op. cit.*, p. 76 f.; GASTER, *op. cit.*, p. 275 f.

[5] Cf. J. WASH WATTS, *A Survey of Syntax in the Hebrew Old Testament* (Nashville,
1951), pp. 6-7.

accomplished in the past (the natural order long since established v 7, and the day which was darkened to night as the people took up their vigil in the sanctuary v 8).

The sequence of tenses is consequent and clear. The worshippers stand between the acknowledged order and events of the past and the great coming event of the morning. The hymn urges preparation for that event (iv 12b) for the issues are life and death, blessing or judgement (v 6). The singer reminds the people that all about them in that night of waiting and in the approaching dawn are signs of Jahweh's work, power, and authority. Preparation for meeting him in the morning begins with the recognition that he is indeed Lord of all, Jahweh God of Hosts.

The tone of the hymn is that of a polemic against Ba'alistic worship. Its radical pronouncement of Jahweh's power and authority claims for him the very functions which were claimed for *Ba'al* in addition to others which would make a comparison of the two unthinkable. This battle for the soul of Israel had raged long before Elijah voiced Jahweh's claim for absolute allegiance in the reign of Ahab. [1] But as Amos spoke the fight was not yet won. This hymn is a part of that battle. Its origin might be found somewhere between Elijah and Amos. Amos' use of it seems to show that it was quite familiar to his audience. It was old enough to have been firmly fixed in the festival's tradition and to have become widely known.

The hymn's themes run parallel to those loved by the prophets. It is like a prophetic psalm. [2] Aubrey Johnson has suggested that cult prophets in ancient Israel were the forerunners of the singing and preaching Levites of a later day. [3] If that be true, the natural group to sing such psalms in preparation for the great ceremonies were the bands of prophets. They were the preachers of repentance, the predictors of the future, the jealous watchdogs of Jahwistic faith. This hymn is both a profession of their faith [4] and a call to faith probably sung in chorus, calling the people to God.

E.   THEOLOGICAL IMPLICATIONS

Such an interpretation and such a dating of this hymn has a number of important implications for the understanding of the history of Israel's faith.

---

[1] I Kings xviii.

[2] GUNKEL, *op. cit.*, pp. 361-379.

[3] A. JOHNSON, *The Cult Prophet in Ancient Israel* (Cardiff, 1944).

[4] CRAMER, *op. cit.*, p. 96; HORST, *op. cit.*, p. 50 f.; GUNKEL, *op. cit.*, p. 276.

It implies a fully formed doctrine of Jahweh as creator prior to Amos. Without going into details, the hymn reveals a deep and complete doctrine which lies behind it. Wind, mountains, the heavenly bodies, and the orderly changes of nature all owe their origin to His creative touch. Thus creation in all its movements witnesses to His thought and purpose. All power and direction derive from Him. Therefore life and hope belong to Him alone.

This witness to a doctrine of Jahweh's creation of the cosmos is all the more important because the earlier, so-called Jahwistic, account [1] does not contain that statement.

The second implication of the hymn is that monotheistic faith and expression predate Amos. [2] In these lines Jahweh is presented as the source of all power and direction. He alone is God, Creator, Sustainer, and Director of all things. Amos' deep conviction that Jahweh was absolute Lord of all was nourished by such hymns as this. He did not originate the doctrine, it was his inheritance.

F. AMOS' USE OF CULTIC MATERIALS

If the interpretation of these verses is correct, they are to be viewed as a Psalm from the Jahwistic cult. In them we have a good opportunity to study a prophet's use of cultic materials.

In the first chapter we saw that Amos was a prophet in every sense of the word and that he may very well have (we might say "he must have") taken a full part in prophetic activities in the cult. In the second lecture we saw that otherwise obscure passages in Amos have both unity and sense when interpreted against the background of the cult. Now we have isolated three strophes of a cult psalm which is quoted in Amos.

Why does such a hymn appear among the speeches of Amos? [3] In ch. 4 the quotation appears after a fairly long passage reciting

---

[1] Gen. ii 4a ff.

[2] MAAG, *op. cit.*, p. 49.

[3] GUTHE, "Der Prophet Amos," *op. cit.*, p. 37 suggests that the doxologies ended various collections of Amos' speeches. BUDDE, *J.B.L.* XLIV (1925), p. 106 disagrees suggesting that they are simply used to fill in for lost speeches of Amos. SELLIN, *Das Zwölfprophetenbuch* (*K.A.T.*, 2nd. ed., Leipzig, 1929), p. 225 thought they occurred wherever the sanctuary at Bethel was denounced. HORST, *op. cit.*, p. 50 explained the doxologies as confessions required in the process of sacred justice. WEISER, *op. cit.*, p. 202 suggests the predominance of the earthquake in Amos' thinking to be responsible for the position of the hymn fragments.

God's earlier chastisements of Israel and her continual refusal to repent. A threat of judgement must have preceded this, for the last line reads: "Therefore thus will I do to you, Israel!" The prophetic speech is complete.

Yet the following lines are joined to the speech by: "Because I will do this to you, prepare to meet your God, Israel." As we have seen above, the latter part seems to be the introductory line of the hymn. Why should these two appear together? Why should they be so joined?

The natural answer would be that they were actually presented in this way. The prophet's speech of judgement led up to the singing of the hymn at its appropriate place in the celebration. The proclamation of Jahweh's judgement was a very natural buildup for the hymn's call to preparation and repentance before Jahweh God of Hosts. [1] One might think of Amos speaking the words of the hymn, but it seems more fitting to think of the prophetic band as picking up the chant or the song at the close of his message. [2]

The hymn is here quoted to fill a necessary part of the picture of Amos' activity. The prophet's message did not stand alone in its original setting. It contributed an important element to the great religious experience of the festival. The prophetic protest against insincere religious observance came from inside, not from outside the religious structure. That it was not supported by all who formed a part of that structure is obvious. [3] But it is equally clear that men like Amos did not simply stand isolated and alone. [4]

The second hymnic quotation is connected with the messages of Amos at two points. In both of them Amos uses a slight variation of the first line of this hymn's second strophe to introduce a message. In v 4 he cries in Jahweh's name, "Seek me and live!" In v 14 he says, "Seek good and not evil, that you may live." In both of these we recognize variations of the hymn's "Seek Jahweh and live." (v 6). [5]

In this instance the hymnic quotation does not document an order of service but indicates the original source of Amos' play on words. [6] His references to this familiar hymn must certainly have been clear

---

[1] Cf. CRAMER, *op. cit.*, p. 93.

[2] *Ibid.*, p. 99; H. SCHMIDT, *Amos*, p. 23.

[3] Amaziah, the priest, for one.

[4] CRAMER, *op. cit.*, p. 99.

[5] MAAG, *op. cit.*, p. 49.

[6] Cf. viii 2 for another play on words.

to the listeners. But they would also have been clear because these messages must have been spoken accompanying that portion of the ritual to which the hymnic strophe fitted. Behind his words lie not only his own will to call the people to repentance, but the matter of ritual necessity. Such a call by a prophet belonged in that portion of the ritual. Does this mean that there is nothing different in Amos from the common run of the prophets? [1] Not at all. But the difference lies in the deadly earnestness of this Judaean and in the power of God which he manifested in his prophecy, not in the simple fact of his call to repentance. This quotation shows us that the prophetic message was supported by elements of the ritual itself as well as by the activity of his fellow prophets.

In Amos' two messages we see how the prophets might pick up a phrase or a motif from the liturgy and expand it to give the particular emphasis needed for that hour. Both of them are in a sense commentaries and clarifications of the original hymnic call. In them Amos makes abundantly clear, what is actually in the hymn but may have been glossed over through constant repetition and familiarity, that not empty ritual but a personal relation, including moral content, is the only valid worship of Jahweh.

The third passage does not have such obvious contact with its context. The context refers to God's having determined ("set his eye" ix 4, 8) upon judgement for Israel. The verse which makes a definite contact with this theme is vs. 6a. Here God is described as "determining his thoughts in the heavens" and establishing them on the earth. This third strophe of the hymn seems to be intended to document this work of God which is the basis for the vision and its succeeding messages. It is Jahweh who determines the fate of all. Now Israel's fate has been decided and was already being put into effect. There had been warnings enough [2] and even divine patience was at an end. This indicates that in this message Amos was using a motif of the cult (New Year's omen) along with the particular language of that cult setting ("Setting God's eye upon one") as the basis for his message of judgement.

In these we can see some hints concerning Amos' use of cult motifs which are documented in the hymn. Often the prophet's words ran parallel to cultic procedure and phrasing, even when his real intention was quite opposite to popular or contemporary under-

---

[1] As is often inferred from the term "cult prophet."
    Cf. Amos iv 6-11.

standing of the cult. He picked up rare portions, like this hymn, which were of true Jahwistic content, even as he derided and condemned cultic practices which were heathen in both form and intent. Amos knew the cult of his day to be syncretistic. He therefore did not hesitate to use its valid portions in the very act of condemning those invalid parts. He repeated the call of the prophetic criers or singers. But he emphasized that this was a call to faith and to faithful obedience, a call to repentance, rather than simply a call to participate in temple rites which more nearly represented the worship of Ba'al than the true worship of Jahweh.

There is one more question to which we must turn. It involves the use of quotations in the literary process by which the prophetic literature was formed. Robert Gordis has published a study of "Quotations in Biblical, Oriental, and Rabbinic Literature." [1] He is primarily interested in Wisdom Literature. But a similar study might be made of the Prophets, as well. [2]

Our study has shown that the first strophe of the hymn in Amos is very closely connected with the text so that responsibility for its quotation might even be placed on the prophet himself. [3] But this is not the case with the other two instances. It is impossible to escape the conclusion that their preservation was determined at the time that the speeches of Amos were being collected to put in a fixed form either oral or written. In this lies a further testimony to the widespread familiarity with this hymn for it is quoted in both parts of the Book, although they were collected in two quite different places. [4]

These collectors (or editors) were careful, then, to preserve those things which would help to make the words of Amos readily understood to generations far removed from the setting in which he spoke. We can only be deeply grateful to them for preserving this example of cultic hymnody in which such important testimonies to the faith and worship of Israel are found.

---

[1] *H.U.C.A.* XXII (1949), pp. 157-219.

[2] H. W. WOLF, *Das Zitat im Prophetenspruch* (*B.E.V.T.* 4, Munich, 1937) deals with quotations in prophetic speech but does not touch these passages. The work here envisioned would go beyond that to treat quotations inserted during the editorial process.

[3] In spite of numerous assertions by scholars to the contrary. Cf., for example, HORST, *op. cit.*, p. 49.

[4] See p. 50.

CHAPTER FOUR

AMOS' ESCHATOLOGY

The possible existence of an eschatology in the thought of eighth-century Israel has been and is a topic for heated discussion. [1] Not a little of the disagreement concerns a definition for eschatology. [2]

There is much more substantial agreement that the eschatology of the Old Testament centers in "The Day of Jahweh." [3] There is also common agreement that the earliest use of this phrase is found

---

* In this chapter the following books have been drawn upon so heavily that adequate documentation would be impossible, and if attempted would surely prove a burden to the reader: L. ČERNÝ, "The Day of Yahweh and Some Relevant Problems," *Prace z Vedeckych Ustavu* (Prague, 1948); H. GRESSMANN, *Der Messias*; H. J. KRAUS, *Gottesdienst in Israel*; S. MOWINCKEL, *P.S.* II and III; V. MAAG, *Text, Wortschatz und Begriffswelt des Buches Amos*; *Id.*, "Jahwäs Heerscharen," *Köhler Festschrift*; C. R. NORTH, *The Old Testament Interpretation of History* (London, 1946); J. PEDERSEN, *Israel* I-IV; H. W. ROBINSON, "The Day of Yahweh," *Inspiration and Revelation in the Old Testament* (Oxford, 1946); N. H. SNAITH, *The Jewish New Year Festival*; ROWLEY, *The Faith of Israel* (London, 1956), pp. 177-202.

[1] Cf. A. S. PEAKE, "The Roots of Hebrew Prophecy and Jewish Apocalyptic," *The Servant of Yahweh* (Manchester, 1931), pp. 95-96: "It must still be regarded as very questionable whether there was in early Israel any developed eschatology at all." TH. C. VRIEZEN, "Prophecy and Eschatology," *Congress Volume, Copenhagen*, 1953 (*S.V.T. I*, Leiden, 1953), p. 199 ff.; S. SMITH, *Isaiah, Chapters XL-LV: Literary Criticism and History* (Schweich Lectures 1940, London, 1944), p. 18. E. J. YOUNG questions the validity of the question itself in saying that the rise of eschatology must be viewed as due to "a special revelation to Israel", *The Westminster Theological Journal* (1949), p. 190; J. LINDBLOM, "The Problem of Eschatology in the O.T.," Paper read at the Society for Old Testament Study, Rome Meeting, April 1952, *Ordo Lectionum* 8th paper; *id.*, "Eschatology in the Prophets," *S.T.* VI (1953), pp. 79-114; E. JACOB, *Théologie de l'Ancien Testament* (Neuchâtel, 1955), pp. 255 ff.

[2] R. S. CRIPPS, *Commentary on the Book of Amos*, pp. 55-64; J. HEMPEL, "The Contents of the Literature," *R.R.*, p. 65; A. C. KNUDSON, *The Beacon Lights of Prophecy* (New York, 1914), p. 55; J. D. W. WATTS, *The Heavenlies of Isaiah* (unpublished dissertation, Southern Baptist Theological Seminary, Louisville, Ky., 1948), p. xix; C. STEUERNAGEL, "Die Strukturlinien der Entwicklung der jüdischen Eschatologie," *B.F.*, pp. 479-487.

[3] A. J. WENSINCK, "The Semitic New Year and the Origin of Eschatology," *Acta Orientalia* I, pp. 169-170; W. A. HEIDEL, *The Day of Jahweh* (New York, 1929); L. I. PAP, *Das israelitische Neujahrsfest* (Kampen, 1933); J. M. P. SMITH, "The Day of Jahweh," *American Journal of Theology*, pp. 505-533.

in the Book of Amos. [1] The question whether the term is truly "eschatological" in Amos [2] may be saved for the end of the investigation.

Only twice does Amos actually use "The Day of Jahweh" (v 18-22). But other references point to it. "That Day" must certainly have the same meaning, [3] while terms like "evil day," [4] "bitter day" [5] are related to it. Reference to "days" which are coming [6] must also be related to the concept. The threatened punishment which in chs. i-ii Jahweh will not "turn back" also fits the picture.

The references in Amos reflect a popular expectation that the Day is coming. [7] Amos agrees and even heightens the expectancy by insisting that it will be "dark" and not "light," [8] a day of "death" instead of "life" [9] or "evil" instead of "good". [10]

A. ORIGIN OF THE DAY

But where did Amos and the people get their common understanding of the Day of Jahweh? [11] And what was the actual form of this concept? [12] Amos pointed to periods and places of festival in

---

[1] Amos v 18-20.

[2] The question is an old one. THOMAS HALL, *An Exposition of Amos* (London 1661) distinguished two days of Jahweh (Cf. ČERNÝ, *op. cit.*, p. 75). W. O. E. OESTERLEY, *The Doctrine of the Last Things* (London, 1909), p. 20 calls it "a well-known *terminus technicus*" the first time it occurs in the Old Testament. GRESSMANN and ČERNÝ agree, but see CRIPPS, *op. cit.*, p. 299 ff.

[3] Amos ii 16, viii 3, 9-10, 13-14; ix 11-12; perhaps iii 14. H. H. ROWLEY, *The Biblical Doctrine of Election* (London, 1950), p. 153, n. 1; P. A. MUNCH, *The Expression bājjōm hāhū* (Oslo, 1936).

[4] Amos vi 3.

[5] Amos viii 10.

[6] Amos iv 2-3; viii 11-12; ix 13-15. Cf. STAERK, *Z.A.W.* XI (1891), pp. 247-253. But notice that there is a clear distinction from "the day" and that the two are neither confused nor allowed to overlap.

[7] G. HÖLSCHER, *Die Ursprünge der jüdischen Eschatologie* (Giessen, 1925), p. 13 contends for an non-eschatological interpretation. NEHER, *Amos* (Paris, 1950), p. 115 f. follows CRAMER in denying popular origin.

[8] Amos v 18-20.

[9] J. LINDBLOM, *Das Ewige Leben* (Uppsala, 1914), pp. 1-2.

[10] Amos ix 4.

[11] Cf. E. SELLIN, *Israelitisch-jüdische Religionsgeschichte* (Leipzig, 1933), p. 63 ff.

[12] From the following references one may gain an idea of the diversity of opinion on the subject: M. BUBER, *The Prophetic Faith*, p. 107; R. H. CHARLES, "Eschatology," *E.B* II, cols. 1348-1354, sections 34-50; B. D. EERDMANS, *The Religion of Israel* (Leiden, 1947), p. 150; A. VON GALL, *Basileia tou Theou* (Heidelberg, 1926), pp. 26-27; L. KÖHLER, *Theologie des Alten Testaments*, p. 79; MOWINCKEL, *op. cit.*, pp. 230-244; MUNCH, *op. cit.*, p. 60, n. 16; J. PEDERSEN, *Israel I-II*, p. 545, n. 1; ROBINSON, *op. cit.*, pp. 135-144; J. M. P. SMITH, *op. cit.*; W. R. SMITH, *The Prophets of Israel*, p. 398; SNAITH, *op. cit.*, p. 69, n. 17; P. VOLZ, *Die Eschatologie der jüdischen Gemeinde im neutestamentlichen Zeitalter* (Tübingen, 1934), p. 63.

Israel. [1] Recent study has recognized the Autumn Festival as the only major national festival observed as a pilgrimage at that time. [2] The only sanctuary with which we can with certainty link Amos is that at Bethel, [3] although it is not impossible that he served elsewhere in Northern Israel [4] and certain that he must have prophesied in some sanctuary in the south. [5] These sanctuaries had some things in common, but they also had distinctive elements which must be identified. [6]

One statement will sum up the general characteristics of ritual in these sanctuaries: *it was a syncretistic mixture of Canaanite and Israelite elements*. [7] But festivals in these sanctuaries were the most important (if not the only major) influence in matters of religion. [8] Whatever content the religion of the people had came from priestly and prophetic [9] ministrations in these sanctuaries. And by far the most influential festival at this period was that in the autumn at which harvest and New Year was celebrated. [10]

Recent archaeological discoveries make possible a fairly comprehensive description of Canaanite ritual for the New Year. [11] The central point and purpose of the festival was the renewal of nature's powers and those of the community. [12] The principal features included:

---

[1] Cf. Hoffmann, *Z.A.W.* III (1883); von Gall, *op. cit.*, p. 24 ff.; A. Weiser, *Das Buch der zwölf Kleinen Propheten* I (*A.T.D.*, Göttingen, 1949), p. 111; A. Bentzen, "The Ritual Background of Amos i 2-ii 16," *O.T.S.* VIII (1950), p. 92; H. Gross, *Weltherrschaft als religiöse Idee im alten Testament*, pp. 149-150.

[2] Cf. use of "the Festival" to designate it: I Kings viii 2, 65; xii 32, 33; II Chr. v 3; vii 8, 9. The idea of pilgrimage emerges in Ju. xxi 19. Cf. A. Alt, "Die Wallfahrt von Sichem nach Bethel," *K.S.*, p. 87.

[3] Amos vii 10-17. See above p. 24.

[4] See p. 18 above.

[5] See p. 34 above.

[6] R. Brinker, *The Influence of the Sanctuaries in Early Israel* (Manchester, 1946).

[7] H. Junker, *Theologie und Glaube* (1935), pp. 686-695, understands Amos v 25 f. to indicate just such a mixture. Cf. S. H. Hooke, "The Myth and Ritual Pattern of the Ancient East," *Myth and Ritual* (London, 1933), p. 5; Nyberg, *Studien zum Religionskampf im Alten Testament*, *A.R.W.* 35 (1938), pp. 329-387.

[8] Cf. R. Brinker, *op. cit.*; S. Mowinckel, *Religion und Kultus*; G. Östborn, *Cult and Canon*.

[9] See p. 3 above notes 4-5 for literature.

[10] Cf. Most recently A. R. Johnson, *Sacral Kingship in Ancient Israel*, p. 49 ff.;

[11] Cf. Geo Widengren, *Sakrales Königtum im Alten Testament und im Judentum*, p. 62 f.; S. H. Hooke, *The Origins of Early Semitic Ritual* (London, 1938); T. H. Gaster, *Thespis*.

[12] Hooke, *Myth and Ritual*, p. 4.

"(a) The dramatic representation of the death and resurrection of the god.

(b) The recitation or symbolic representation of the myth of creation.

(c) The ritual combat, in which the triumph of the god over his enemies was depicted.

(d) The sacred marriage.

(e) The triumphal procession, in which the king played the part of the god followed by a train of lesser gods or visiting deities." [1]

In such ritual the worshippers expected to be assured that the fruitful forces of nature would fulfill their desires during the coming year. They shared with their gods the good things of the harvest just past and expected to share with them the victories, renewal, and fruitfulness enacted in the ritual. [2] The ritual thus assured "good fortune" in the coming year.

One should however note, at this point, that the ritual is not all one of joy and light. The first three elements, at least, contain representations of death, [3] of chaos, of enemies of their fruitful god. [4] Victory is not won without striving, battle, and a goodly share of ritual magic.

Although the elements of divine death [5] and sacred marriage could not be accepted by any true Israelite, there is abundant evidence that these practices continued in Israel down to the Exile. [6] However, it is doubtful whether their direct antithesis to Jahwistic doctrine would allow them to figure as principal features of the cult. [7] The other three elements (creation, ritual combat, and triumphal procession) could have been easily adapted to quite legitimate usage in a Jahwistic ritual. [8]

Jahwistic contribution to this syncretistic ritual must also have been one of cult. Recent studies have given us a picture of Israel's worship prior to the kingdom which centered in periodic festivals

---

[1] *Ibid.*, p. 8.

[2] GASTER, *op. cit.*, p. 3 ff.

[3] J. MORGENSTERN, "Amos Studies III", *H.U.C.A.* XV (1940), pp. 284-285.

[4] MOWINCKEL, *Religion und Kultus*, p. 72.

[5] MOWINCKEL, *op. cit.*, p. 70.

[6] References to the practice of ritual prostitution are found in II Kings xxiii 7, Ez. viii, I Kings xiv 24, xv 12, xxii 46, Dt. xxiii 17.

[7] MOWINCKEL, *op. cit.*, p. 77.

[8] Cf. JOHNSON, *Sacral Kingship in Ancient Israel*.

of covenant renewal. [1] The center of such celebration seems to have been Shechem, although the central symbol of this worship was the Ark of the Covenant. [2]

The elements of this service may be traced in Joshua 24 and Exodus xix-xxiv: (a) recognition of Jahweh as electing, saving, leading God of Israel in a summary of his *historical* relation to Israel; [3] (b) the demand for absolute loyalty to Jahweh alone, for he is a jealous God [4] (including cleansing the people of false worship of other gods); [5] (c) the people's express agreement; [6] (d) the reading of the conditions of covenant (law and promise); [7] (e) final ceremonial agreement to the covenant as well as the preservation of a testimony to it. [8]

A clear contrast existed with the emphases of Canaanite cult. [9] Jahweh was Lord and he addressed the people always from that exalted position. [10] His primary realm was history. [11] The purpose of the renewal was not repetition of covenant-making, but actualizing of the God-People relation by allowing the people to re-experience the original covenant ceremony. [12] Jahweh came and judged the people on the basis of the covenant. [13] Repentance and confession on the part of Israel were met with cleansing and forgiveness on the part of Jahweh. [14] The heart of this covenant was God's election and God's law, representing both his promise and his

---

[1] Cf. M. NOTH, *Das System der zwölf Stämme Israels* (Stuttgart, 1930); G. VON RAD, *Das formgeschichtliche Problem des Hexateuchs* (Stuttgart, 1938); A. WEISER, *Die Psalmen I* (*ATD* 14, Göttingen, 1950), pp. 18-29; J. HEMPEL, *R.R.*, p. 73; N. SNAITH, *R.R.*, pp. 251-258.

[2] Ex. xix 4-6, xx 2; Joshua xxiv 2-13.

[3] KRAUS, *op. cit.*, p. 125 and C. NORTH, *op. cit.*, p. 125 stand solidly opposed to MOWINCKEL's "historization of myth" hypothesis.

[4] Ex. xx 3-6; Joshua xxiv 14-15.

[5] Joshua xxiv 23.

[6] Ex. xix 8, xxiv 7; Joshua xxiv 24, xvi 22. KRAUS, *op. cit.*, p. 47-49.

[7] Ex. xxiv 3-7; Joshua xxiv 25.

[8] Ex. xxiv 4-8; Joshua xxiv 26-27.

[9] Cf. above pp. 2-3.

[10] Ex. xx 1; KÖHLER, *op. cit.*, p. 12 f.

[11] J. RIEGER, *Die Bedeutung der Geschichte für die Verkündigung des Amos und Hosea* (Giesen, 1929); C. R. NORTH, *The Old Testament Interpretation of History* (London, 1946), p. 141 ff.

[12] M. NOTH, "Die Vergegenwärtigung des Alten Testaments in der Verkündigung," *Ev. T.* XII (1952), pp. 6-16.

[13] The centrality of the covenant idea in the work of the 8th century prophets has recently been noted by B. DAVIE NAPIER, *From Faith to Faith* (New York, 1955), p. 175.

[14] M. BUBER, *The Prophetic Faith*, p. 104.

demand. [1] And one last feature must be mentioned: the covenant was "mediated" by one who spoke for God, pronouncing his law, seeking forgiveness, and bringing about agreement. [2] The particular scene of Amos' activity was Bethel. [3] This ancient sanctuary had traditional relation to the Patriarchs [4] and was again mentioned in relation to Samuel's activities. [5] Jeroboam I chose it as an official pilgrimage sanctuary for the Northern Kingdom giving it prestige and royal favor. [6] He reestablished the cult there, setting up a golden bull as the central cult object. [7] Although the bull seems to have had ancient connections with Jahweh worship, [8] there is no denying that it stood as a fertility symbol. [9] As such it demonstrated more clearly than any words the tendency toward Canaanite practice. [10] It was presented with the words: "Behold your gods, O Israel, who brought you up out of the land of Egypt." [11] Here Jeroboam laid claim to the name "Israel" [12] for his kingdom as well as claiming Jahweh's election which went with it. [13] He took his place on the foundation of the old amphictyony. [14]

It should also not escape our notice that he established a Fall Festival for Israel [15] and installed royally appointed priests for Bethel's ritual. [16] This royal connection is attested also in Amos. [17]

References in the historical books tell of the importance of Bethel

---

[1] W. EICHRODT, *Theologie des Alten Testaments* Teil I (4th ed., Berlin, 1950), p. 7.

[2] M. NOTH, "Das Amt des Richters Israels," *B.F.*, p. 404 ff.

[3] Amos vii 10-17. Cf. M. Bič, "Bet'el—le sanctuaire du roi," *Archiv Orientalni* 17 (1949), pp. 46-63.

[4] Genesis xii 8; xii 3; xxviii 19; xxxi 13; xxxv 1-16.

[5] I Sam. vii 16; x 3.

[6] I Kings xii-xiii.

[7] W. F. ALBRIGHT, *From the Stone Age to Christianity* (2nd. ed., Baltimore, 1946), p. 229 f.

[8] Ex. xxxii 1-6.

[9] J. PEDERSEN, *Israel III-IV*, p. 639: "The image of the bull denoted that Yahweh's nature was associated with the ox which formed the centre of Canaanite life and worship."

[10] L. ROST, "Stierdienst," *R.G.G.* V (2nd. ed.), col. 803.

[11] I Kings xii 28.

[12] L. ROST, "Sinaibund und Davidsbund," *T.L.Z.* (1947), col. 131.

[13] Cf. Amos iii 2.

[14] That the attempt was not without difficulties may be seen in the portrayal of NOTH, *Geschichte Israels* (Göttingen, 1950), pp. 201-2.

[15] T. OESTERREICH *Reichstempel und Ortsheiligtümer in Israel (Beiträge zur Förderung Christlicher Theologie*, Gütersloh, 1930).

[61] R. H. KENNETT, "The Origin of the Aaronite Priesthood", *J.T.S.* VI (1905), pp. 151-186.

[17] Amos vii 13.

through the following century and a half. [1] Amos and Hosea attest to its importance in their day. [2]

Bethel, then, was an illustration of the syncretism sketched above. Such a syncretistic festival must have contained the following elements.

(a) Jahweh was celebrated as Creator [3] including great accounts of his control of nature. [4]

(b) The hoped-for renewal of nature (including the coming of rain) was celebrated through theophanic accounts of Jahweh's providential care. [5]

(c) Ample opportunities for exciting representations of Ritual Combat [6] were afforded by the dramatization of Jahweh's freeing Israelites from Egypt and their taking the Land of Canaan.

(d) Whereas a truly Canaanite festival reached its peak in the sacred marriage, an Israelite festival must have climaxed in a celebration of Jahweh as Lord of the Covenant. [7] At appropriate intervals (perhaps even annually) [8] this must have been a ceremony of covenant renewal. [9] But whether the actual renewal took place or not, Jahweh appeared at the climax of the festival as Israel's Covenant God, her Lord, her Saviour, [10] her King. [11] As such he judged her for her sins, especially for any unfaithfulness to him through the worship of other gods. [12] Having purged his people, [13] his will was re-expressed through his law. [14] With the covenant again secure through God's purging action and forgiving mercy, pronouncement of blessing with all of its assurances of salvation, plenty, and peace was possible.

---

[1] II Kings ii 2-3; x 29; xvii 38; ch. xxiii.

[2] Amos chs. iii-v; vii 10-17; Hos. x 15; xii; A. ALT, "Die Wallfahrt von Sichem nach Bethel", K.S. I, pp. 79-88.

[3] JOHNSON, op. cit., p. 53ff.

[4] H. W. ROBINSON, Inspiration and Revelation in the Old Testament, p. 17ff.

[5] Cf. above, p. 41 f.

[6] ČERNÝ, op. cit., p. 77.

[7] Cf. above, p. 9.

[8] Dt. xxxi 10 speaks of a seven-year interval.

[9] ROWLEY, op. cit., p. 76 ff.

[10] JOHNSON, op. cit., p. 125.

[11] M. NOTH, "Gott, König, Volk," Z.T.K. (1950), p. 157 ff.; A. ALT, "Gedanken über das Königtum Jahwehs," K.S. I, pp. 345-357; MORGENSTERN, op. cit., pp. 284-285; HOOKE, Myth and Ritual, p. 10.

[12] VOLZ, op. cit., p. 93.

[13] Thus leaving the righteous remnant. Cf. von GALL, op. cit., p. 30 ff.

[14] Cf. the order of Joshua xxiv 25-28. A. ALT, Die Ursprünge des Israelitischen Rechts (1934), K.S. I, p. 278-332.

(e) The triumphal procession then celebrated Jahweh's reign over his people as well as his victory over all his enemies.

From this point on, of course, the festival was one of celebration and joy in the nature of harvest festivals. [1] Canaanite stress on harmony with nature's forces taught a mythical and cyclic view of time in which renewal was always necessary and simply repeated the unending cycles of existence. [2] But Israel's faith was grounded in history. Time was viewed as linear, not cyclic. [3] Her election and salvation were based on great acts of God which happened once and could never be repeated. These two differing concepts of time and reality created a tension of self-contradiction within the cult, as well as in the thinking of the people.

The "Day of Jahweh" must have been understood in both ways. It was an apt description for that high point of the festival and for God's goal in history.

As celebrated within the cult, the "Day of Jahweh" centered in Jahweh's *coming*, [4] his *judgement*, and his *decree* [5] of acceptance or rejection of his people. Judgement was not a final decision, but preparation for the final decree. Therefore judgement took the form of chastisement unto repentance [6] or of expiation of sinful elements from the people. [7] It was then possible for the decree affecting the "remnant". [8] of the people to be one of renewed blessing within the covenant. [9] This was the "happy ending" longed for by the people.

As expected in history, "that day" must contain the same elements in which judgement would be a purgative and expiatory preparation for the decree of lasting salvation, peace, and blessing for a surviving remnant.

Renewal of the covenant required a "mediator" who could speak God's will to the people. [10] This involved both an office and a

---

[1] GASTER, *Thespis*, p. 27.

[2] MOWINCKEL, *Religion und Kultus*, p. 70.

[3] C. R. NORTH, *The Old Testament Interpretation of History*, pp. 124-5.

[4] Cf. von GALL, *op. cit.*, p. 26, n. 3; G. PIDOUX, *Le Dieu qui vient* (Neuchâtel, 1947), pp. 14 f.

[5] Note the difference between "judgements" cited in Amos iv 6-11 and the "decrees" of vii 8 and viii 2.

[6] J. BRIGHT, *The Kingdom of God*, p. 88.

[7] A. S. KAPELRUD, "God as Destroyer in the Preaching of Amos and in the Ancient Near East," *J.B.L.* LXXI (1952), pp. 33-38.

[8] H. H. ROWLEY, *The Faith of Israel*, p. 117 f.

[9] S. R. DRIVER, *Joel and Amos*, p. 185.

[10] ALT, "Die Ursprünge des israelitischen Rechts", *K.S.* I, p. 324.

charisma. [1] If the king or the priest filled the office, [2] the place of the charismatic speaker still had to be filled. The prophet, called and inspired of God, was such a man. It is probably in exactly that position that we should picture Amos' ministry.

Another note to this cultic celebration must be added. We have observed that Amos served both in Judah and in Northern Israel. [3] In the Judaean service one added feature must have weighed heavily in thoughts concerning the covenant. Beside the Covenant of Sinai stood that with David. [4] Judaeans would long since have impatiently awaited the day when Jahweh would make good his promise of restoring to the "son of David" [5] rulership over "all Israel" [6] along with the glory promised for that rule.

One final factor remains to be mentioned. Periods of distress in Israel must have raised the question in people's minds as to whether this was the historical reality of judgement portrayed in the cult. [7] The eighth century B.C. presented to the pious Israelite ample opportunity to ask if the threatening gestures of a growing Assyrian Empire were not signs that God's purge of nations pictured in the cult was now forming on the stage of history. [8]

At that point in history and against the background of Bethel's ritual, a man was called of God to announce His will to Israel. [9] His name was Amos.

B. AMOS' MESSAGE

In his first vision (vii 1-3) Amos was given to see a plague of locusts which like other such catastrophes (iv 6-12) was intended to chastise Israel and bring her to repentance. Although this plague failed in its purpose (iv 9), the prophet interceded for Israel and was able to pronounce God's decree recalling the judgement.

---

[1] KRAUS, *Gottesdienst in Israel*, p. 61 ff.; M. NOTH, "Das Amt des 'Richters Israel'." *B.F.*, p. 404 ff.

[2] L. KÖHLER, "Die hebräische Rechtsgemeinde," (1931) reprinted in *Der hebräische Mensch* (Tübingen, 1953), p. 159 ff.

[3] Cf. above p. 25, n. 5 and p. 34.

[4] ROST, *op. cit.*, p. 130; ROWLEY, *op. cit.*, p. 98 ff.

[5] E. SELLIN, *Die israelitisch-jüdischen Heilserwartungen* (1909); Id., *Der alttestamentliche Prophetismus* (Leipzig, 1912), pp. 102-193.

[6] ROST, *Israel bei den Propheten* (Stuttgart, 1937), p. 102 ff.; G. A. DANELL, *Studies in the Name Israel in the Old Testament* (Uppsala, 1946), p. 288 ff.

[7] An example of past events so interpreted may be found in Amos iv 6-11.

[8] ALBRIGHT, *From the Stone Age to Christianity*, p. 240.

[9] Amos i 1; vii 15.

His second vision (vii 4-6) contemplated a "judgement by fire." [1] This figure fits most nearly the purging ordeal through which Israel might be both tested and cleansed. But survival for Israel did not come because she was able to brave the ordeal, but only through God's merciful response to the prophet's intercession. Amos i 2-ii 16 presented an extended message in which fire from Jahweh appeared repeatedly. [2] Jahweh came, and as the Lord of History came he purged the nations. [3] Jahweh's coming was specifically to Israel, so the prophet turned finally to her. [4] Her sins were laid bare. [5] Sin was placed in the proper context through a reminder that Jahweh had given them the land, had rescued them from Egypt and raised up those who might continue to mediate his blessings to them. But all these had been ignored. Therefore Jahweh would shake them to their very foundations with a judgement which no man could escape. [6]

The speech fitted perfectly the task of the Jahwistic spokesman announcing the coming of Jahweh on the great day of the Festival. [7] Jahweh's voice was coming from Zion and was directed toward worshippers in northern sanctuaries. [8] The sermon recognized sins of history [9] and of society. Social and moral degeneracy [10] was closely linked with empty worship. [11] But at this point there was no forward look to impending *historical* judgements. [12] This judgement was to be accomplished within the cult service and one may assume that the effective intercession of the prophet made possible the restoration of blessed covenant relations and the joyous continuation of the festival. [13]

---

[1] W. F. ALBRIGHT, *B.A.S.O.R.* 62 (1936), pp. 30-31; H. J. KRAUS, "Der Gerichtsprophet Amos—Vorläufer des Deuteronomisten", *Z.A.W.* L (1932), pp. 221-239.

[2] Amos i 2, 4, 7, 10, 12, 14; ii 2, 5.

[3] Judgement over the nations is a common motif: H. GROSS, *Weltherrschaft als religiöse Idee im Alten Testament.*

[4] Amos ii 6-16.

[5] In greater detail, more specifically, and individually than for the others.

[6] Amos ii 13-16.

[7] J. LINDBLOM, "Wisdom in the Old Testament Prophets," *Wisdom in Israel and in the Ancient Near East (S.V.T.* III, Rowley Festschrift, 1955), p. 202.

[8] Amos i 2.

[9] W. COSSMANN, *Gerichtsgedanke bei den alttestamentlichen Propheten*, p. 4; Amos i 3, 6, 9, 11, 13; ii 1.

[10] Amos ii 6-7a; iv 1; v 11-13; vi 4-7, 12; viii 4-6.

[11] Amos ii 7b-8; iv 4-5; v 5, 21-23.

[12] Amos ii 13-16 gives no indication of specific historical prediction.

[13] Cf. W. A. IRWIN, *The Old Testament: Keystone of Human Culture* (New York, 1952), pp. 175-76.

The third vision (vii 7-8) recorded a sharp change. Jahweh established a standard of judgement in Israel and forestalled any possibility of prophetic intercession. The short summary of the prophet's message that followed (vs. 9) is purely a description of destruction on the level of history. High places, sanctuaries, and the house of Jeroboam would be pillaged and laid waste. It is in the "words" belonging to this period [1] that the "Day of Jahweh" is consistently pictured as dark and without light. The validity of worship in the sanctuaries was scorned, [2] and the announcement of a decreed [3] historical judgement (defeat, [4] destruction, [5] and exile [6]) was laid bare. Israel's punishment had been decreed on the basis of her privileged position and responsibility of election (iii 2). The threatening evil would be sent of God (iii 3-6) and announced by his prophet (iii 7-8). The Lord had laid Israel open and defenceless before her greatest enemies and summoned them to take their prey (iii 9-11). There could be no talk of Israel's salvation as the "remnant" (iii 12) [7] for cult would fall with the social structure *on that day* (iii 13-15). Both socially elite (iv 1-3) and religiously zealous (iv 4-5) would be caught up in this destruction which all Israel had earned through repeated refusal to repent in the face of chastisement (iv 6-13).

The decree was fixed and the prophet could intone Israel's funeral dirge [8] (v 1-2). That day would see the forces of Israel literally decimated (v 3). The issue was one of survival. Three appeals to the people to "seek Jahweh", seek "good", and reestablish justice and righteousness, served to emphasize the utter futility of sanctuary and ritual at that moment (v 4-5, 14-15, 21-24). The people's nefarious injustice and lack of mercy had earned this "evil time." (v 10-13). The judgement would fall when Jahweh passed through their midst (v 16-17). The evil decreed for "that day" was inescapable and the day would be "darkness and not light" (v 18-20). Those who were indifferent or blindly overconfident (vi 1-8) were castigated for their

---

[1] Amos chs. iv-vi especially v 18-20; Cf. above p. 47 ff.
[2] Amos iv 4-5.
[3] Amos iii 9.
[4] Amos ii 1-3; iii 8, 14.
[5] Amos vi 11.
[6] Amos iv 2-3; v 5; vi 7.
[7] An idea which depends upon continued covenant relations for its validity.
[8] A category used fairly often by the prophets: A. BENTZEN, *Introduction to the Old Testament* (Copenhagen, 1948), p. 137.

failure to see and care for Israel's ruin. Their lack of common sense and caution was inexcusable (vi 12-13), and the passage closed on a repeated announcement of coming military defeat and subjection (vi 14).

In these passages the judgement which was announced was clearly not to be experienced in the cult. [1] It was not simply a preparation for the great climax of the festival. [2] The very validity of sanctuary and cult was denied. [3] Sin was judged as having broken the bonds of the covenant and invalidated covenant institutions. [4] Therefore the society which was supported by the covenant, both politically and religiously, was doomed. Language from the cult was still used. [5] Punishment was described as "when I pass through your midst." [6] But the stark reality would be in history and had the tone of finality in that it would mark the end of the "Israel" which the Northern Kingdom claimed to be. [7]

The fourth vision and the speeches connected with it (ch. viii) returned to cultic setting and language. [8] But its contents ran parallel to those of the previous section. "The end" had been decreed upon the relation which the festival cult celebrated. [9] Therefore the change of seasons, (vs. 8) the signs for that day (vs. 9) lead to grief instead of joy. But the distress which followed would not be simply material but also spiritual in that God could not be found nor his blessings obtained (vs. 11). The organs of the covenant-relation (cult, priest, prophet) had been removed or disowned (vs. 12).

It has sometimes been thought that the references to the sun going down at noon (vs. 9) were sure indications of a cosmic eschatology which pictured the end of the world. [10] But this cannot

---

[1] The references in iv 6-11 start this trend.

[2] Note references to places and battles in Amos vi 2.

[3] Amos v 5, 21-22.

[4] Amos vii 8 and the implied denial of permission for prophetic intercession.

[5] Amos v 1-2, 6-9.

[6] Amos v 17. A. ALT, "Das Königtum in den Reichen Israel und Juda," *V.T.* I (1951), p. 2 ff.

[7] ČERNÝ, *op. cit.*, p. 81-82, suggests that which was not truly eschatological before became so when the fate of the whole nation was at stake. The explanation of the origins of eschatology purely in terms of historical necessity does not explain why earlier crises of this nature, like the Philistine pressure under Samuel, did not produce an eschatology.

[8] Cf. above p. 26 ff.

[9] "My people" Amos vii 8. Hosea i 9 expresses the break by the name: "Not my people."

[10] Cf. NORTH, *op. cit.*, pp. 126-127.

be. The figure is one common to theophanies [1] and most appropriate to the cultic description of "the day" as light or dark (vs. 18). But this passage, as distinct from chs. i-ii, does portray a judgement touching the cult which bears marks of finality (vss. 2b, 14), futurity (vss. 3, 8-14), and comprehensiveness (vs. 3: "my people Israel") like that in chs. iii-vi. One is pictured in the harsh terms of history, the other in cultic terms. But they must otherwise be put into the same category in regard to expected fulfillment. This fulfillment in both cases lies outside the possible experience of the cult.

The fifth vision (ix 1-4) depicted the giving of an order which accomplished decreed judgement (vs. 4b). The scene was laid in a sanctuary (ix 1). Perhaps what Amos saw as the Lord commanding shattering of pillars was the earthquake mentioned in i 1. [2] But the continued description goes far beyond the work of an earthquake in describing the thoroughness with which Jahweh's judgement would affect all of them. [3] This, like ii 14-16, emphasized that this judgement was inescapable. Judgement would be a kind of ordeal intended to purge out rebellious and profane elements from the people. "All of them" (ix: 1) certainly needed further definition. After a verse (vs. 7) in which "Israel", stripped of her covenant privilege, was put on a par with other peoples, the object of judgement was defined as "the sinful kingdom" (vs. 8b) and all the sinners of my people" (vs. 10). Amos carefully stated that not all the house of Jacob (or Israel) would be destroyed, but that it would be sifted so that the sinners should perish (vs. 9). This certainly fitted the concept of a purgative judgement which should make possible the reestablishment of Jahweh's covenant relation with his people.

"That Day" would make possible the rehabilitation of David's, house and kingdom which should possess the territory promised to him (vss. 11-12). [4] The hope of reestablishing David's kingdom, which was an important element of Judah's faith, stood in the key position dominating the scene. [5] All the previous verses of the

---

[1] H. W. ROBINSON, "The Nature-miracles of the Old Testament," *Inspiration and Revelation in the Old Testament*, pp. 39-43.

[2] J. MORGENSTERN, "Amos Studies I," *H.U.C.A.* XI (1936), p. 140.

[3] Cf. BUBER, *op. cit.*, pp. 107.

[4] ROWLEY, *op. cit.*, pp. 151-152; J. LINDBLOM, "The Political Background of the Shiloh Oracle," *Congress Volume: Copenhagen* 1953, pp. 78-87; J. SCHMIDT, *Der Ewigkeitsbegriff im Alten Testament* (Münster, 1940), p. 163.

[5] M. NOTH, "Jerusalem und die israelitische Tradition," *O.T.S.* VIII (1950), pp. 28-46.

chapter built toward this announcement for "that day". But these latter verses (11-12) make no mention of "Israel", only David. The hopes for Israel were spoken in terms of a reversal of her decreed fate (*šūb šĕbūth*) [1] which must yet be accomplished in that distant future ("behold days are coming" [2] vss. 13-15). There was no mention of the restoration of cult or kingdom. These gave way to the prior claims of Zion and David. Hope lay in the promise of "the Land." That hope applied to "all Israel" [3] just as the amphictyonic covenant established in Jerusalem and as the Davidic kingdom did.

C. "DAY OF JAHWEH" IN AMOS

Amos viewed the "day of Jahweh" from three standpoints. The ritual celebration of the day presented a number of inherent implications and possibilities which are reflected in Amos.

1. Jahweh's relation to surrounding nations implied his wider rule and authority. [4]

2. Celebration of Jahweh as creator [5] laid the basis for a conception of his work at the beginning of the world and thus implicitly at the end of the world.

3. Judgement was understood in terms of Jahweh's coming [6] and explained in three stages: chastisement to repentance, [7] expiation through ordeal, [8] and finally a decree announcing acceptance or rejection of the people and of the covenant by Jahweh. [9]

---

[1] E. L. DIETRICH, **שׁוּב שְׁבוּת** *Die endzeitliche Wiederherstellung bei den Propheten* (*B.Z.A.W.* 40, Giessen, 1925).

[2] ROWLEY, *op. cit.*, p. 152; *Id., The Growth of the Old Testament* (London, 1950), pp. 82-83.

[3] G. A. DANELL, *Studies in the Name of Israel in the Old Testament* (Uppsala, 1946); L. ROST, *Israel bei den Propheten* (*B.W.A.N.T.*, 4th Series 19, Stuttgart, 1937); W. EICHRODT, *Israel in der Weissagung des Alten Testaments* (Zürich, 1951); G. VON RAD, "Israel," *T.W.N.T.* III (1938), pp. 357-359.

[4] Amos chs. i-ii; ix 6.

[5] Amos v 7-9.

[6] Amos v 17.

[7] Amos iv 6-11.

[8] Amos ii 13-16; v 6, 16-20; vii 4-6; viii 11-14; ix 1-4, 9-10.

[9] Amos vii 3, 6, 8; viii 2; ix 8, 11. Cf. SNAITH, *op. cit.*, p. 72.

4. Celebration of covenant in the ritual implied at least a knowledge of Jahweh's ethical demands. [1]

5. The celebration of judgement left open the possibility of a final decree of rejection, although a positive decree was expected. [2]

6. Cult validity depended upon two things: the free decision of Jahweh, Israel's transcendent, sovereign God, [3] and his acts in history through which this covenant had been established. [4]

Amos never developed or realized *all* these "eschatological" implications of the ritual. [5] But he did work within the framework of this cult in *proclaiming Jahweh's coming for the high day of the Festival*. His concept in chs. i-ii was plainly centered in the ritual [6] and can hardly be called "eschatological" in any sense.

Amos as a true Jahwistic prophet did stress the theological and ethical elements of the ritual more and with greater vigor than one would expect of a prophet in Bethel. This stress upon the ethical nature of the covenant he also applied fully to the Day of Jahweh. Although this element was implicit in the covenant ritual, Amos' words would hardly be so distinctive in the Old Testament if all those who filled that role took these ethical requirements so seriously as he. He understood election as dependent upon realization of the ethical implications of the Covenant in the life of the people. [7] He insisted that ritual presentation must correspond to living reality [8] and *vice versa*. Jahweh was Lord of all life, as well as of the cult.

Because the people's life was primary to Jahweh, Amos expected

---

[1] Amos ii 10-11; iii 2.

[2] Covenant and its renewal always implies the possibility of rejection. Cf. N. SNAITH, *The Distinctive Ideas of the Old Testament* (Philadelphia, 1946), p. 136.

[3] Amos iii 2; v 15; v 21-24; vii 8; viii 2.

[4] Amos ii 9-10; ix 11.

[5] Can it be that in the North this tended toward a kind of "realized eschatology" of bountiful prosperity, while the South held fast to an historical goal made explicit in the promises to David?

[6] Cf. CRIPPS, *op. cit.*, p. 55.

[7] W. S. McCULLOUGH, *J.B.L.* LXXII (1953), p. 254.

[8] G. A. F. KNIGHT, "Eschatology in the Old Testament," *S.J.T.* 4 (1951), pp. 355-362.

nature and history to be the primary stages on which he worked.[1] Therefore the cultic drama had to reflect the true situation in life. Historical redemption and covenant were reflected in the cult. Natural catastrophes which plagued the people were real enough and represented chastisements in history to turn the people to God. [2] The cultic picture of a purged and renewed "People of God" must find its real expression in the actual life of the people. [3] If it did not, the cultic experience was empty and meaningless, [4] and the result which the cult foresaw for such an eventuality must find its expression in history. [5] *The Day of Jahweh was to be the time when that which the cult pictured would find realization or fulfillment in historical reality.* The "dark" or "evil" day of the cult would be reflected in the defeat, destruction, and exile of sanctuaries and kingdom.

Yet this historical viewpoint was further interpreted through cultic picture when this *end* decreed upon Bethel's "Israel" was presented as expiation which made possible the reestablishment of Zion's "Israel." *He interpreted the historical Day of Jahweh in terms of election, covenant, judgement, and telos as presented in the cult.*

If what Amos described may be called "eschatology", how is it to be defined? We have seen that there were implied seeds of eschatology in the cult which were *amphictyonic* (concerning "all Israel"), *supranational*, [6] and *cosmic*. Amos developed only the first. Only Israel came within his view, and the concern of his "eschatology" was the establishment of the true "Israel."

His interpretation of the "Day of Jahweh" summed up his view. It was to be the *end* of the Northern Kingdom's claim to the Covenant and its promises. But it was to be neither the end of the world, nor of history. [7] Even the term "end of the age" may be too strong. For Amos it meant the "coming" of Jahweh in judgment to remove persons and conditions which obstructed accomplishment of his

---

[1] MOWINCKEL (*P.S.* II, p. 231) assumes the opposite. ROBINSON (*op. cit.*, p. 133 f. and p. 142) is certainly right that eschatology cannot simply be the product of the ritual, but does he not undervalue the role of ritual in providing the frame of reference?

[2] Cf. ČERNÝ's necessary correction (p. 91) of MOWINCKEL's underplaying the nature catastrophies (p. 222). In Amos iv 6-11 they seem to have been real enough.

[3] A. ALT, "Die Heimat des Deuteronomiums," *K.S.* II, p. 269.

[4] Amos iv 4-5; v 21-23.

[5] HÖLSCHER, *op. cit.*, pp. 13-14.

[6] Cf. CRIPPS, *op. cit.*, p. 56.

[7] B. D. EERDMANS, *The Religion of Israel*, p. 140.

purpose. This would open the way for him to fulfill promises to Israel and to David.

Election which operates on the plane of history implies *telos* (a goal). [1] Wherever history is interpreted in terms of an elective *telos* one should expect a kind of eschatology describing that goal and God's means of achieving that goal. That we have in Amos.

---

[1] Cf. A. C. WELCH, *Jeremiah: His Time and His Work* (London, 1928), p. 119. The prophets did not begin with history. "They began from Yahweh, whose character and whose standards they knew, and whose perfect will could not fail to bring about his end."

SUBJECT INDEX

INDEX OF AUTHORS

EXEGETICAL INDEX